Cipollone v. Liggett Group

Suing Tobacco Companies

Diana K. Sergis

Landmark Supreme Court Cases

Enslow Publishers, Inc.

40 Industrial Road   PO Box 38
Box 398   Aldershot
Berkeley Heights, NJ 07922   Hants GU12 6BP
USA   UK

http://www.enslow.com

Library of Congress Cataloging-in-Publication Data

Sergis, Diana K.
Cipollone v. Liggett Group : suing tobacco companies / Diana K.
Sergis.
      p. cm. – (Landmark Supreme Court cases)
Includes bibliographical references and index.
ISBN 0-7660-1343-X (alk. paper)
1. Cipollone Rose, d. 1984—Trials, litigation, etc.—Juvenile literature. 2. Liggett & Myers
Tobacco Company—Trials, litigation, etc.—Juvenile literature. 3. Trials (Products
liability)—United States—Juvenile literature. 4. Tobacco—Products liability—United
States—Juvenile literature. [1. Cipollone, Rose, d. 1984—Trials, litigation, etc.
2. Liggett & Myers Tobacco Company—Trials, litigation, etc. 3. Tobacco industry.]
I. Title. II. Series.
KF228.C52 S47 2001
346.7303'8—dc21
      00-009787

To Our Readers:
All Internet Addresses in this book were active and appropriate when we went to press. Any
comments or suggestions can be sent by e-mail to Comments@enslow.com or to the address
on the back cover.

Photo Credits: American Cancer Society, pp. 44, 103; Centers for Disease
Control, Office on Smoking and Health, pp. 13, 23, 24, 96; Courtesy of Ness,
Motley, p. 9; Department of Health and Human Services, Public Health Service,
pp. 30, 32; Photofest, p. 8; *Star-Ledger* Photos, pp. 37, 48, 61, 72, 76; Supreme
Court Historical Society, p. 80.

Cover Photo: Corbis Images Royalty-Free

Contents

This book is lovingly dedicated to my family: To my late father, Kyriakos, who encouraged me to dream and to follow my dreams; to my mother, Euterpi, who taught me to love books and story-telling; to my sisters, brother, nieces and nephews, brothers-in-law and sister-in-law, and family of friends for their love and support; and most especially to my sister and best friend, Carol, without whose research and unfailing guidance this book would not have been written.

Acknowledgments

The author wishes to acknowledge and thank: Barbara Moss of *Star-Ledger* Photos for her help with some of the photo research; Lisa Funston of Ness, Motley for her diligence in tracking down photos of Rose and Antonio Cipollone; Nicole Blair of the Centers for Disease Control for the loan of her slide of the seven tobacco executives at the 1994 Congressional Subcommittee hearing; and to Marguerite Stratton and Carol Tomassini for their constructive critiques of my original manuscript and for their encouragement.

"To cease smoking is the easiest thing I ever did. I ought to know, I've done it thousands of times."

—Mark Twain

Author's Note

Reading about the *Cipollone* case, you may question Rose Cipollone's reasons for suing the tobacco companies. After all, she was the one with the long-term, self-destructive smoking habit. Was her lawsuit merely about money? Or would her day in court help to bring about needed changes in the tobacco industry? Would it change the way the industry promoted and marketed its products? Would it help force the industry to reveal information about the ill effects of cigarettes to the public?

In hindsight, Rose Cipollone's downward spiral started long before her doctor found a spot on her lung in 1981. (Three years later, she died of lung cancer.) She, like millions of other teenagers, became a victim of appealing cigarette advertising, peer pressure, and nicotine addiction. (Nicotine is a poisonous, habit-forming substance used as an active ingredient in cigarettes.)

How much of the responsibility for Rose Cipollone's lung cancer was hers? Should we blame the victim, as the tobacco industry did? Should we blame the tobacco industry as the Cipollones did? Or should the responsibility be shared?

You may also question the tactics of the cigarette makers (not their reasons, for they were unquestionably driven by a desire to make a profit). Here, you must apply an important underlying factor: that cigarette ad campaigns have misled the public and promoted the smoking habit. The tobacco industry allegedly knew about the health dangers of cigarette smoking early on and hid the evidence. For too long, the tobacco industry denied that cigarettes are harmful or addictive. It would not recognize that the Cipollone family and all cigarette smokers have legal rights and protections.

Keep in mind that the federal government is not without blame either. Has its unwillingness to enforce rules for the tobacco industry been solely a constitutional matter of states' rights versus federal rights? Or, does the federal government have other reasons for its unwillingness to enforce rules against the tobacco companies?

Introduction

Rose Cipollone was a typical teenager in the early 1940s. Cigarette ads during that time featured glamorous movie stars. She could not help but notice these ads prominently placed on billboards and splashed across the pages of newspapers and magazines. She could not help but hum along to the catchy jingles played in cigarette commercials on her favorite radio stations. (Most American homes did not have television sets until the late 1940s and early 1950s.) Some of her favorite actors and actresses puffed away on cigarettes in movie roles. Wouldn't she be tempted to smoke? After all, she would want to look glamorous, too.

Rose Cipollone (born Rose Defrancesco in 1925) started smoking cigarettes at age sixteen. She claimed she was seduced by the glamorous ads. "I thought that it was cool to smoke, and [act] grown up," she explained, "and I was going to be glamorous or beautiful."[1]

She said she was first influenced by ads for Chesterfield cigarettes that glamorized smoking. Later, other ads reassured her, and many other smokers, that cigarettes were safe. Would the issue of ad campaigns hold up in court?

What ever became of Rose Cipollone's dreams and

Bette Davis was one of the glamorous movie stars of the 1940s who smoked. This picture of her from around 1949 shows her smoking.

fantasies? Like a cloud of smoke rising from her lit cigarette and vanishing into the air, the glamour of smoking proved to be a cruel trick for her. Smoking's addictiveness, however, took hold and held fast. She continued to smoke for the next forty years.

Cipollone did not stop smoking when she developed a smoker's cough, an early warning sign that something was wrong. She did not stop in 1981, when she was diagnosed with lung cancer. Even after Cipollone had a lung removed in 1982, she continued to smoke in secret. Rose Cipollone finally stopped smoking in 1983. One year later, she was dead.

Keep in mind that cigarette smoking was socially acceptable in the 1940s, when Rose Cipollone lit up her first cigarette, and continued to be accepted into the early 1960s. It would take the stern warning of the United States Surgeon General in 1964 to alert Americans to the dangers of smoking. Health warning labels would not actually appear on cigarette packages until 1966—almost twenty-five years after Rose Cipollone first started smoking. Did Cipollone know about the dangers of smoking, and if so, when?

Could Cipollone, in fact, have stopped smoking? Can a smoker choose to stop at any time, or is a smoker a helpless victim? The lively debate continues. Despite mounting medical evidence of the addictive effects of nicotine, some people are still not convinced of nicotine's habit-forming nature.

In 1983, Rose Cipollone and her husband, Antonio, filed suit against Liggett, Philip Morris, and Lorillard. These three tobacco companies made the brands Rose Cipollone had smoked throughout her life. The couple blamed these companies for luring Cipollone into a lifelong smoking habit and for her cancer. Rose Cipollone, in particular, felt strongly that the tobacco companies had betrayed her trust in them.

On October 21, 1984, Rose Cipollone died in her husband's arms from lung cancer.

Rose and Antonio Cipollone filed suit against Liggett, Philip Morris, and Lorillard in 1983. The Cipollones are shown here in or around 1947.

She was fifty-eight years old. She left behind a loving, shattered family—her husband, three children, and grandchildren.

Though overmatched, the Cipollone family fought its way through the complex United States court system with some degree of success. There were many twists and turns along the way in this complex case. The Cipollones battled the tobacco companies despite countless delays and mounting legal costs. Where one family member left off, another would continue the legal action.

The legal theories used by the Cipollones' attorneys at times clashed with either state or federal laws. Various interpretations of these laws also caused many setbacks and produced some unanswered questions. For the Cipollones, it was a nine-year legal battle that ended in the United States Supreme Court, the highest court in the nation.

1

Big Tobacco

The tobacco industry has historically been treated well by the federal government. Until the *Cipollone* case, tobacco makers had successfully defended themselves in lawsuits against smokers' damage claims. The tobacco companies had financial resources and political power, which they used to their advantage. But just how did the tobacco industry become so powerful?

Tobacco's Historical Importance

Tobacco held an important position in the early history of the United States. During the seventeenth and eighteenth centuries, tobacco was an important crop in the Southern colonies. American colonists used it as a "cash crop" to buy other goods and services. During the American Revolution (1765–1783), colonists used tobacco as a down payment for loans from France, to help finance the war. The image of a tobacco leaf was stamped on money used in the American colonies.

Taxes on tobacco and cigarettes helped the nation raise needed money for two wars. Congress taxed tobacco for the first time in 1862 during the Civil War (1861–1865). To help raise money to fight the Spanish-American War (1898), Congress raised taxes on cigarettes 200 percent.[1]

Wartime also provided the tobacco industry with a great opportunity to spread the use of tobacco and later, the cigarette habit. Starting with the Civil War in America, tobacco was given out to soldiers in the North and the South. During wars that followed, the United States military gave out free cigarettes to its servicemen and women. This practice did not end until 1975.[2]

In 1864, cigarettes were rolled by hand in the first American cigarette factory. James Bonsack's invention of a cigarette-rolling machine in 1881 made production faster. A Bonsack machine could produce one hundred twenty thousand individual cigarettes a day.[3] The high volume of production made cigarettes widely available at relatively affordable prices.

Since then, cigarette production, sales, and company profits have risen at extraordinary rates. From 1900 to 1924, sales of individual cigarettes in the United States went from 4.4 billion to 73 billion. The amount of individual cigarettes produced in 1996 alone totaled 760 billion.[4] The

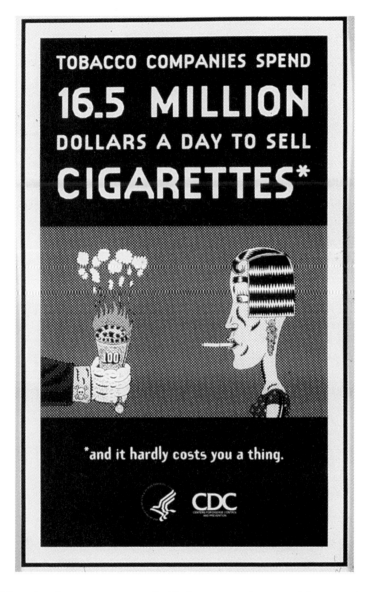

The sale of cigarettes is a profitable business in the United States. From 1900 to 1924, sales of individual cigarettes in the United States went from 4.4 billion to 73 billion.

number of cigarette packages sold and taxed in 1996 was 87.7 billion.[5]

Government Aid to Tobacco Industry

The federal government has financially supported the tobacco industry to some degree. The financial support began in the 1930s, a time known as the Great Depression. It was a period of major economic crisis in the United States. Responding to the crisis, Congress enacted many of President Roosevelt's "New Deal" policies. Because of the overproduction of tobacco and low tobacco crop prices, the federal government provided economic relief to tobacco farmers. From 1933 to 1981, various government programs paid tobacco farmers to reduce their crops and to convert some of their farmlands to other uses that conserved the soil. The federal government also lent farmers money to store their tobacco until market prices rose. Government assistance in the tobacco industry was well established by the time Rose Cipollone came along.

The Rise of Liggett, Philip Morris, and Lorillard

Rose Cipollone sued the three tobacco companies she claimed were responsible for her lung cancer. They were Liggett (makers of Chesterfield and L&M cigarettes), Philip Morris (makers of Virginia Slims and Parliament), and Lorillard (makers of True). Together, they represented powerful opponents in the Cipollones' legal battle.

Most smokers are probably unaware of the companies that make and sell their brands of cigarettes. Yet together, the histories of those companies span over two hundred forty years of American culture and business. Here is a brief look at the origins of Liggett, Philip Morris, and Lorillard and where they rank today.

Liggett Group, Inc.

Liggett Group, Inc., is the smallest of the five major tobacco companies in the United States today. (In ranking order, the five major tobacco companies in the United States are: Philip Morris, R.J. Reynolds, Brown & Williamson, Lorillard, and Liggett.) It started out as J.E. Liggett & Brother in 1873 and incorporated as Liggett & Myers Tobacco Company in 1878. Liggett did not make cigarettes until the 1890s. The Chesterfield brand (the one Rose Cipollone first smoked) was introduced in 1912.

Philip Morris

Philip Morris set up a corporation in New York in 1902 to sell its British brands. In 1929, it bought a factory in Richmond, Virginia, and began making its own cigarettes. Today, Philip Morris is the largest cigarette maker in the world.

Lorillard

Lorillard is the oldest tobacco company in the United States. Its founder, Peter Lorillard, opened a factory for processing tobacco in 1760. At that time, tobacco was used for pipes, cigars, and snuff. (Snuff is a crushed tobacco that is inhaled through the nostrils.) Today, Lorillard is owned by the Loews (theater) Corporation.

1995 Market Share (in percents)[6]				
Philip Morris	RJR	B&W	Lorillard	Liggett
46.1	25.7	18.0	8.0	2.2

Influence of Cigarette Advertising

Cigarette makers promoted their products to national audiences through ads in movies, on radio and television, and in newspapers and magazines. The influence of cigarette advertising on the American public was powerful.

Hollywood movies in the 1930s and 1940s portrayed smoking as glamorous. In recent times, however, Hollywood has been criticized for promoting the smoking habit. A study found that 80 percent of male and 27 percent of female lead characters smoked in top moneymaking movies from 1990 to 1996.[7]

Cigarette sponsorship of radio shows, and later, television shows, brought cigarettes directly into America's homes. Philip Morris, for example, sponsored the popular *I Love Lucy* television series when it began in 1951. Cigarette advertising on radio and television would continue unregulated for the next twenty years. Cigarette ads were banned from airing on television in 1971 but continue to appear in newspapers and magazines.

The message of a cigarette ad was (and still is) a persuasive sales tool. Liggett introduced Chesterfield cigarettes in 1912 with the slogan, "They do satisfy." In 1926, Chesterfields targeted women in an ad that read, "Blow some my way." In 1933, an ad in the *New York State Journal of Medicine* boldly claimed that Chesterfields were "just as pure as the water you drink . . . and practically untouched by human hands."[8] Another persuasive sales tool was the use of famous people to promote particular brands of cigarettes. Through the years, the message and the image presented in cigarette ads became sleeker and more captivating.

Tobacco Industry Counters Health Scare

The tobacco industry also used ads to counteract health warnings about cigarette smoking and to calm the public's fears. Evidence shows that the tobacco industry knew about the ill effects of smoking as early as 1953. Dr. Ernst Wynder, a Liggett scientist, performed experiments on mice by painting cigarette tar on their backs. (Tar, a residue in tobacco smoke, consists of poisonous chemicals that collect in the smoker's lungs.) Wynder's 1953 report said that some of the mice developed tumors and died.

Rather than make this important finding public, the tobacco industry ran a two-page ad, called "A Frank

Statement to Smokers," in over four hundred newspapers. The ad said there was no proof that smoking caused cancer.[9]

Rose Cipollone's attorneys submitted Wynder's report and the ad at trial along with many other tobacco company documents and cigarette ads as evidence. Her attorneys claimed this type of evidence proved that the tobacco companies had concealed knowledge that smoking was linked to cancer.[10]

In the mid-1950s, published health studies connected smoking with lung cancer. Tobacco companies quickly began marketing filtered cigarettes with reduced levels of tar and nicotine.[11] Not surprisingly, sales of these cigarettes soared. An advertising war of low tar and nicotine soon developed among various tobacco companies.

In February 1960, the Federal Trade Commission (FTC) announced a ban on the tobacco industry's unfounded health claims of low tar and nicotine in their advertising.[12] The FTC, created in 1914, is an independent agency of the federal government. Its purpose is to ensure fair trade competition. Among its responsibilities, the FTC regulates the packaging and labeling of consumer goods to prevent false advertising.

The Tobacco Institute (a group formed in 1958 by the tobacco industry) tried to influence the medical community. It distributed a tobacco industry magazine, *Tobacco and Health (Research)*, to doctors at no cost.

According to Judge H. Lee Sarokin, the trial judge in the

Cipollone federal case, this magazine was self-serving at best. The tobacco industry recognized, Sarokin explained, "that smokers would look to their doctors for advice and that many doctors were smokers themselves. . . ." The real purpose of the magazine, he said, was "to convince doctors that the claimed risks [of smoking] were unfounded, unsupported or refuted."[13]

It was not until the mid-1960s, however, that the general public started to become aware of the health hazards of cigarette smoking. Then the mounting evidence from medical journals and health officials could no longer be ignored. Perhaps most influential was the Surgeon General's report in 1964. The Surgeon General, as head of the Public Health Service, stated in the report that cigarette smoking "is a hazard."[14]

Influence of the Tobacco Lobby

Lobbying is the attempt to influence lawmakers. The right to petition, which is guaranteed by the First Amendment to the Constitution, guarantees the right of special interest groups to lobby lawmakers. The tobacco industry has historically been a powerful lobby, or influence, on lawmakers.

Time and again, the tobacco industry tried to block the federal government's attempts to put restrictions on its activities. The tobacco industry has used a combination of effective methods, including denial, delay, and compromise.

- To help pass the Food and Drug Act of 1906, Congress struck a compromise with representatives from tobacco states such as North Carolina, Kentucky, and Tennessee. In exchange for their support of the proposed plan, the word "tobacco" would not be included in the government list of drugs. (In addition, the 1934 Garrison Law that outlawed marijuana and other drugs did not include tobacco as a drug.)

- The compromise would later affect attempts by the Food and Drug Administration (FDA) to regulate tobacco. The FDA, a federal agency created in 1927, is part of the Public Health Service. It ensures the safety of foods, drugs, and cosmetics that are sold to the public. It also ensures that labels and packaging of these products are truthful. However, the issue of whether the FDA has authority over the tobacco industry would be argued for many years. Beginning in 1995, this issue became a fierce, ongoing court battle. At that time the FDA attempted to rule that nicotine, the active ingredient in cigarettes, was a drug. (See Chapter 7.)

- When the Federal Communications Commission (FCC) proposed a ban on cigarette ads on radio and television in 1969, the cigarette companies lobbied vigorously against it. (The FCC, a government agency created in 1934, regulates radio, television, wire, and cable communications.) A compromise was struck. In return for a delay in federal controls on the sale of cigarettes, the cigarette makers agreed to stop advertising on television and radio.

- The actual ban on cigarette broadcast advertising went into effect two years later. It came as a result of the Cigarette Smoking Act of 1969, which amended the Cigarette Labeling and Advertising Act of 1965. However, cigarette companies can and still do advertise their products in newspapers and magazines.

- The tobacco industry also tried to block local laws that were tougher than state laws or restrictions. It supported the enactment of state tobacco control laws, such as New Jersey's in 1982, that would be more powerful than local laws.

Tobacco Industry's Deep Pockets

The influence of special interest groups on American politics became even stronger when the Federal Election Campaign Act of 1971 allowed corporations to form political action committees (PACs). PACs contribute money in support of political parties and candidates. The tobacco industry has made generous political contributions to protect its interests. From 1986 through 1996, it gave about $30.6 million in political contributions.[15] In return, the tobacco companies hoped that Congress and government regulatory agencies would keep a hands-off policy.

One example of how the tobacco industry's strategy paid off occurred in 1994. The FDA received a letter signed by 124 members of the House of Representatives. In it, they criticized the agency for its proposal to regulate tobacco as a drug. The House members said regulation would put thousands of jobs at risk and "trample First Amendment rights to advertise legal products to adults."[16] An identical letter to the FDA was signed and sent by thirty-two senators.

The House members who signed the 1994 letter received an average of $19,446 from tobacco lobby groups, compared to $6,728 for those who did not sign it. Similarly, those senators who signed the letter received an average of $31,368 in contrast to $11,819 for those who did not.[17]

Tobacco Fuels the American Economy

There is no doubt that the tobacco industry is important to the nation's economy. The tobacco companies earn billions of dollars from the sales of tobacco products, especially cigarettes. Federal, state, and local governments also earn billions of dollars from taxes on these products and from industry workers who purchase other goods and services.

A study done on the tobacco industry's impact on the nation's economy in 1994 found that:

- The tobacco industry generated $44.7 billion to the nation's economy.

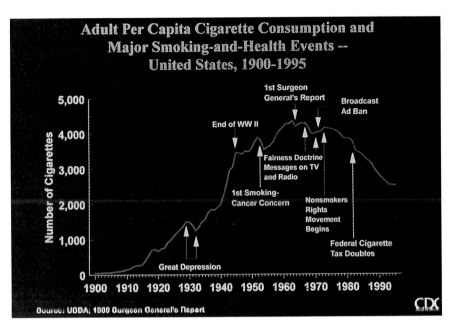

There is no doubt that the tobacco industry is important to the economy of the United States.

- The tobacco industry supported 662,402 jobs.

- Federal, state, and local taxes (on cigarettes alone) totalled $20.6 billion.[18]

- By 1996, the tobacco industry's hold on American and foreign markets was firmer than ever.[19]

- Tobacco crops were grown in twenty-one states and in Puerto Rico.

- Tobacco, the seventh largest cash crop, was worth $2.9 billion.

- 130 billion cigarettes were exported to 130 countries.

- 2.8 billion foreign cigarettes were imported.

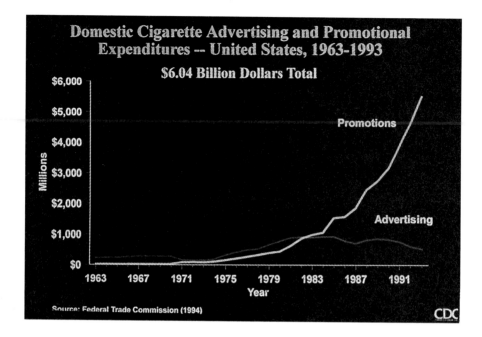

Domestic Cigarette Advertising and Promotional Expenditures -- United States, 1963-1993

$6.04 Billion Dollars Total

Source: Federal Trade Commission (1994)

CDC

The tobacco industry spends a great deal of money every year promoting its products.

With its long history of economic and political power, the tobacco industry has made the same argument repeatedly to the courts and lawmakers. It says the tobacco industry is necessary to the American economy and, therefore, should not be regulated.

However, a basic conflict exists when economic profits become more important than health concerns for the public about smoking. Does everyone really benefit? Do smokers like Rose Cipollone have legal rights? Some smokers who blame the tobacco companies for their smoking-related diseases have taken the companies to court.

2

Building a Case

Rose Cipollone was not the first person to sue a tobacco company for a smoking-related illness. The 1950s and 1960s represented the "first wave" of tobacco lawsuits brought by individual smokers. The 1970s were not marked by more tobacco lawsuits but rather by some tighter regulations on the tobacco industry. The 1980s marked the "second wave" of tobacco lawsuits, with the *Cipollone* case leading the way.[1]

"First Wave" of Cigarette Lawsuits—1950s and 1960s

In the 1950s and 1960s, many lawsuits were filed by dying smokers or their families against the tobacco industry. These smokers failed to win their cases however, for the following reasons:[2]

- The smokers used legal theories that were hard to prove.

- The tobacco companies used delaying techniques that prolonged the time the cases spent in court, up to twelve years.

- The court delays used up the smokers' (or their law firms') money in legal fees. Lack of money and enthusiasm forced the smokers to drop their lawsuits. In comparison, the tobacco companies had plenty of money to continue their strong defenses for years.

- There was a lack of medical evidence available at that time to definitively link cigarette smoking to disease.

- The addictive nature of nicotine (an ingredient of tobacco) was not fully understood in the 1950s and 1960s.

In 1954, the nation's first two smoking liability cases against cigarette companies were filed in federal courts. A liability is a broad legal term applied to debts or obligations for which someone is responsible. In other words, smokers were suing the tobacco companies in hopes that the companies would have to pay for their part in producing a product that harms those who use it.

Pritchard v. *Liggett & Myers* was the first tobacco liability lawsuit.[3] Otto Pritchard claimed that smoking Liggett's

Chesterfield cigarettes had caused his lung cancer. He said that Liggett had advertised the health benefits of smoking this brand of cigarettes. The ads he identified included ones that stated, "Chesterfields are best for you" and "Chesterfields are as pure as the water you drink and the food you eat."[4] The trial court in Pennsylvania said that Pritchard had to prove he relied on such ads when he purchased these cigarettes.

Pritchard appealed, or asked a higher court to review the lower court's decision. In 1961, the appeals court said a jury should decide whether Liggett was liable for not living up to its advertising promises and for failure to test the cigarette product. Pritchard, however, could not prove that Liggett's ads had influenced him to purchase these cigarettes. After twelve years of litigation (legal proceedings), Pritchard dropped the lawsuit.

Cooper v. *R.J. Reynolds Tobacco Co.* was the nation's second smoking liability case.[5] Eva Cooper sued on behalf of her late husband Joseph Cooper, who had died from lung cancer. She charged that the Camel cigarettes he had smoked caused her husband's death. Camel is a brand made by R.J. Reynolds. A federal court in Pennsylvania dismissed Cooper's claim in 1956, because she was not able to state which specific ads had influenced her husband to smoke Camels.

In the early 1960s, legal action against tobacco companies

was also unsuccessful. Seven tobacco liability suits were filed in 1963. Here are two of these cases.

Lartigue v. *R.J. Reynolds Tobacco Co.* involved a longtime smoker.[6] Frank Lartigue started smoking Picayune cigarettes at age nine. Later, he smoked Camel cigarettes. After Lartigue developed cancer of the voice box and a lung, he died at age sixty-five. Lartigue's wife, Victoria, sued on his behalf. She charged that the tobacco company should have warned consumers that its products caused cancer. A federal jury in Louisiana found in favor of R.J. Reynolds. When Victoria Lartigue appealed, an appeals court supported the court's judgment. In 1963, the United States Supreme Court did not agree to hear the case.

In *Ross* v. *Philip Morris Inc.*, John Ross sued the cigarette maker.[7] Ross claimed the cigarettes he smoked had caused his lung cancer. A federal jury in Missouri was not convinced, however. In 1962, after considering the verdict for only one hour, the jury found in favor of Philip Morris. The case was appealed in 1964, but again was decided in favor of Philip Morris. The tobacco company had successfully argued that it was not liable for the harmful substances found in cigarettes. Its reason? It did not know about or could not have known about them.[8]

These early liability cases raised several issues and arguments. The Cipollone family would later use these same arguments (and others) in its court battles.

- **Breach of express warranty** (used in the *Pritchard* case) is a violation of a written or oral promise made by the seller to the buyer. The seller expressly, or specifically, assures the quality or description of the goods being sold.

- **Deceit, or fraudulent misrepresentation** (used in the *Cooper* case) occurs when someone (such as a tobacco company) knowingly deceives or tricks another person (such as a smoker). The deceived party must be ignorant of the true facts and must have relied upon the false statements. As a result, that party is harmed or injured.

- **Negligence** (used in the *Lartigue* case) is the failure of one party (such as a tobacco company) to use reasonable care in its conduct toward another party (such as a smoker). As a result, the second party (in this case, the smoker), may be harmed or injured.

- **Breach of implied warranty** (used in the *Ross* case) is the seller's violation of an indirectly stated promise that the goods are suitable for the purpose required. (Ross had argued that Philip Morris knew or should have known that its cigarettes contained harmful substances.)

29

As Surgeon General in 1964, Luther Terry issued his historic "Report on Smoking and Health." The report found that smoking caused enough serious risks to smokers' health to warrant action being taken.

Surgeon General's Report Sends Shockwaves

Surgeon General Luther L. Terry issued his historic "Report on Smoking and Health" in 1964. It was based on thousands of medical reports and health articles that a special advisory committee had studied. The report concluded that, "Cigarette smoking is a health hazard of sufficient importance in the United States to warrant appropriate remedial action."[9] In other words, smoking caused enough serious risks to smokers' health that action should be taken.

The Surgeon General serves as the nation's leading spokesperson on public health issues. He or she is an assistant secretary for health in the Department of Health and Human Services. The Surgeon General also serves as head of the Public Health Service and the Commissioned Corps (a unit of medical and health professionals).

Why was Surgeon General Terry's 1964 report so

important? It was the first official government recognition of the health hazards associated with cigarette smoking. (As of 1998, there had been twenty-five Surgeon General's reports issued on the subject of smoking and health.) The report was a major news story in 1964. It brought national attention to the health risks of smoking.

The advisory committee's call for action was not specific. Yet, the report had almost immediate reaction in the public and private sectors. Here are some important results.

- More than 30 million Americans quit smoking in the year following the report. Smoking declined steadily thereafter. The number of adults (aged eighteen and over) who smoked went down from 42.4 percent in 1965 to 24.7 percent (a decrease of about 48 million adults) in 1997.[10]

- The Federal Cigarette Labeling and Advertising Act was passed in 1965.[11] It went into effect the following year. This law required cigarette makers to include a simple warning label on all cigarette packages (but not on cigarette advertising). The warning label read:

"Caution: Cigarette Smoking May Be Hazardous to Your Health."

- The number of liability cases filed in 1964 jumped from five the previous year to seventeen.

Yet again, the tobacco industry defendants in these lawsuits

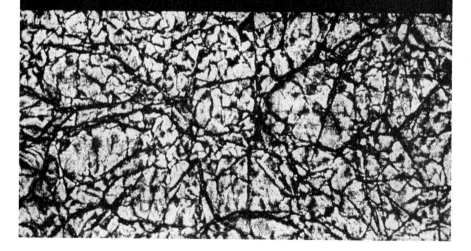

SMOKING *and* HEALTH

REPORT OF THE ADVISORY COMMITTEE
TO THE SURGEON GENERAL
OF THE PUBLIC HEALTH SERVICE

U.S. DEPARTMENT OF HEALTH, EDUCATION, AND WELFARE
Public Health Service

The cover of Surgeon General Terry's historic 1964 report is shown here.

came up with what was to become a winning defense. (A defendant is a person who is sued in a civil lawsuit or the person accused of a crime in a criminal prosecution. A plaintiff is the person who is suing someone else in a civil lawsuit.) This time, they argued that the smokers had an "assumption of risk."[12] This legal concept means that if an individual knows and fully understands the risks of harm from smoking, yet still chooses to smoke, that individual cannot profit from any harm caused by smoking.

How would smokers have had knowledge of the risk? The tobacco companies said the labels on cigarette packages warned them.

Big Tobacco Hides Behind Warning Labels

The Federal Cigarette Labeling and Advertising Act of 1965 contains one critical section that essentially makes the federal labeling law superior over any state or local laws on that subject. (State or local laws would tend to make the warning labels more specific or stronger.)[13] The tobacco industry argued that, in effect, this section of the 1965 Labeling Act gave it immunity (complete protection) against liability. The tobacco company defendants in the *Cipollone* case would make the same argument.

Four years later, the Labeling Act of 1965 was changed by the Cigarette Smoking Act of 1969.[14] The 1969 Act required the warning label to read:

"Warning: The Surgeon General Has Determined that Cigarette Smoking Is Dangerous to Your Health."

The 1969 law continued to protect cigarette advertisers by prohibiting states from creating a ban on regulating cigarette ads for "health-related reasons."[15]

Was Rose Cipollone Warned?

Like millions of Americans, Rose Cipollone had heard about the Surgeon General's report in 1964. She recalled that her husband brought it to her attention. (In fact, Antonio Cipollone did not like her smoking and had always wanted her to quit.[16])

Rose Cipollone had noticed the warning label on her cigarette packages that first read (in 1965):

"Caution: Cigarette Smoking May Be Hazardous to Your Health."

She was asked to recall her reaction to it in her deposition on February 28, 1984. (A deposition is a formal interview that takes place before a trial.) Cipollone testified, or declared under oath, she thought the warning meant "that smoking was dangerous."[17]

Yet, Rose Cipollone continued to smoke because she did not believe she would get lung cancer as a result of her habit. "I was sure that if there was anything that dangerous that the tobacco people wouldn't allow it and the government wouldn't let them," she said.[18]

When Cipollone was asked whether the warning label

had any effect on her smoking, she said, "It didn't make any impact on my smoking, but it did frighten me a little."[19]

Rose Cipollone's reaction to the warning labels may seem casual or indifferent, but it was not uncommon. The FTC reported to Congress in 1967 that "[t]here is virtually no evidence that the warning statement on cigarette packages has had any effect." Part of the reason for this, the FTC said, was that "cigarette advertising continues to promote the idea that cigarette smoking is both pleasurable and harmless."[20]

Rose Cipollone had not noticed the 1970 change in the warning label that read,

> "Warning: The Surgeon General Has Determined that Cigarette Smoking *Is* [italics added] Dangerous to Your Health."

She explained in her testimony that "I didn't open the package and look at the warning every time I smoked a pack of cigarettes."[21]

Almost twenty years after the first warning label went into effect, Congress passed the Comprehensive Smoking Education Act of 1984.[22] It provided for four different health warning labels to be used (and changed in a regular order) on cigarette packages and advertisements. These warnings were more specific about smoking-related health risks. Listed as Surgeon General's Warnings, they read:

> "Smoking Causes Lung Cancer, Heart Disease and May Complicate Pregnancy."

"Quitting Smoking Now Greatly Reduces Serious Risks to Your Health."

"Cigarette Smoking Contains Carbon Monoxide."

"Smoking by Pregnant Women may Result in Fetal Injury, Premature Birth, and Low Birth Weight."

Rose Cipollone did not have the benefit of these warnings in the twenty-three years that she had smoked prior to their existence. Yet, she testified that she tried to quit smoking while she was pregnant with her first child in 1947. She claimed she made this effort only at the urging of her husband and her doctor. "My husband begged me to," she explained, ". . . and I thought oh, I'm going to be so good that I will not smoke and endanger my child or myself, and, of course, [every] once in a while, I'd sneak a cigarette."[23] (Rose Cipollone gave birth to her daughter, Maria, on October 25, 1947.)

At the trial, attorneys for Liggett Group (the defendants) argued that Rose Cipollone *did* know of the dangers of smoking as early as 1947. They brought into evidence a song that was a national hit in 1947. The song was called "Smoke! Smoke! Smoke! (That Cigarette)." It included the lyric: "Puff, Puff, Puff, And if you smoke yourself to death. . . ."[24]

Nicotine Addiction Argument

By 1988, scientific evidence of the addictive nature of nicotine in tobacco could no longer be ignored. On May 16, 1988, Surgeon General C. Everett Koop issued a report on

Surgeon General C. Everett Koop announces the latest report on smoking as he holds a newspaper advertisement placed by the tobacco industry to counter the report.

the health consequences of smoking. This was the first such report to target the fact that nicotine in tobacco is addictive. Dr. Koop stated that cigarettes and other tobacco products were "addicting in the same sense as are drugs such as heroin and cocaine."[25] (The FDA, however, would not declare nicotine a drug until 1995, seven years later.)

Not surprisingly, the Tobacco Institute (a lobby group for the tobacco industry) criticized Dr. Koop's report on two issues. First, the tobacco lobby said that the report played down the importance of "the serious drug problem faced by society." Second, it said that arguments that smokers were addicts "defy common sense and contradict the fact that people quit smoking every day."[26]

Dr. Koop's report helped Cipollone's attorneys argue the issue of nicotine addiction during the trial. Sections of the report were read to the jury.

"Second Wave" of Cigarette Lawsuits Begins: 1980s

There were well over one hundred lawsuits filed by smokers against tobacco companies in the 1980s. These smokers had the benefit of medical evidence that linked cigarette smoking to a variety of diseases. However, most of the individuals did not have the benefit of the cigarette makers' internal documents to use as evidence against the companies in court.

Could Rose Cipollone's attorneys convince the jury in the *Cipollone* case that the tobacco companies were responsible for her cancer? How would they do it?

3

The Road to the Supreme Court

Marc Z. Edell, the lead attorney for the Cipollones, first met Rose Cipollone in the summer of 1983. He had tried to talk her out of a lawsuit against the tobacco companies. He explained that the case would require much of her time and energy. Keep in mind that Cipollone was battling lung cancer during this period. Edell's other concern was that the tobacco companies would try to turn up any personal information they could use against her in court.[1]

Cipollones File Lawsuit

Nevertheless, on August 1, 1983, Rose Cipollone and her husband, Antonio, filed a lawsuit against Liggett Group, Inc., Philip Morris Inc., and Lorillard (the three tobacco companies that made the different brands of cigarettes Rose

Cipollone had smoked over the years). The couple sought damages for the suffering and loss of money resulting from Rose Cipollone's lung cancer. (She had been diagnosed with lung cancer two years before.)

The Cipollones' lawsuit was based on product liability. Product liability is the legal responsibility of makers and sellers for defective or harmful products. It also holds them responsible for the damages caused by the use of dangerous products. In other words, if the three tobacco companies were found liable because their cigarettes were judged defective in a court of law, they would have to pay the Cipollones for damages and for their suffering.

The Cipollones based their lawsuit on four claims.[2] These claims, for the most part, had been tested in courts in the first wave of lawsuits against tobacco companies (see Chapter 2).

- strict liability (tobacco companies were liable for a defective product);
- negligence (tobacco companies failed to use reasonable care);
- intentional tort (tobacco companies committed a willfully wrongful act); and
- breach of warranty (tobacco companies violated their advertising promises).

The Cipollones filed their civil lawsuit in the federal district court in Newark, New Jersey. A civil lawsuit does not deal with criminal behavior. The losing party in a civil lawsuit may be ordered to pay money to the winner, to stop doing something, or to do something to correct a problem. In a criminal case, the person found guilty of a crime is subject to a jail sentence and/or a fine.

A civil case may be tried in either a federal court or a state court. The Cipollone case was brought to a federal court because it dealt with a federal law—the Federal Cigarette Labeling and Advertising Act of 1965.

Depositions at Pretrial Phase

In the pretrial phase, attorneys for the plaintiffs and attorneys for the defendants are busy preparing their cases through discovery. Discovery is a search for information and documents relating to the case. One or both parties in a civil trial may conduct it. During the discovery process, parties exchange information through a written question-and-answer exercise. They then proceed to take depositions, or formal interviews, with witnesses. The witnesses must testify under oath and are cross-examined, or questioned by the opposing party.

Rose Cipollone gave four days of depositions. Because she was very ill, the interviews were spread out over a three-month period (January through March 1984). Cipollone claimed she was intimidated by the group of lawyers representing the three tobacco companies.[3] (At the trial, there would be a total of nine trial attorneys from New York and

41

Washington, D.C., law firms for the defense. They also had legal staff and public relations support available to them.) As Rose Cipollone sat with her attorney, Marc Edell, she seriously considered dropping her lawsuit. But she decided against it. Edell recalled that "[Rose] said if she could stop one person from starting to smoke that it was worth it."[4]

During depositions, lawyers for Liggett, Philip Morris, and Lorillard asked Cipollone many in-depth questions about different aspects of her personal life. They asked her about her family and friends—their names, addresses, dates of birth, dates of death. Cipollone tried to answer each question as best she could. But in many instances, she could not remember specific dates and addresses. It is clear from the transcripts of her depositions that Rose Cipollone had very little energy. She was undergoing chemotherapy, a strong chemical treatment for her cancer, during this period.

As she responded to the tobacco attorneys' questions about herself and her family, Rose Cipollone disclosed her family history. Her parents were both born in Sicily, Italy. Her father, Phillip Joseph DeFrancesco, came to the United States around 1905 at age fifteen. He returned to Sicily in 1921 and married. Then he brought his new bride, Concetta, to New York. They had four children—three daughters and one son.

Rose DeFrancesco, the second oldest child, was born at home on December 17, 1925. She was a happy child who loved to sing and to play the piano. In her early teens, Rose's passions were movies and movie stars. She enjoyed cutting out magazine pictures of movie stars for her scrapbook.

Rose Cipollone and her family lived in one area of New York City from 1926 to 1940. During that time, they lived in a six-room apartment, which was heated by a coal stove in the kitchen. Her father, a barber, died of a stroke in 1940 at age fifty. Rose quit high school in 1942 to go to work at a local variety store. "We were poor," she said.[5] For the next five years, she had a series of clerical jobs.

She met her future husband, Antonio, at a festival in 1946, and they married on February 2, 1947. They had three children: Maria, Thomas, and Rosalina. By all accounts they were a loving, close-knit family.[6]

Back at the offices of Marc Edell's law firm, the tobacco company attorneys questioned Rose Cipollone over and over again about her health history and her smoking habits. Cipollone's testimony revealed that she did not quit smoking when her health was getting worse.

Cipollone recalled that she had developed a smoker's cough during the 1960s. This condition worried her because "there were reports that smoking was unhealthy and caused cancer . . . and I was afraid."[7] She claimed that she had tried to cut down on her smoking at this time, but it was too difficult for her to quit altogether.

From 1947 (when she first tried to quit smoking) to the mid-1960s (when she tried to quit again), Cipollone made no other attempts to quit smoking. Rose Cipollone testified that "tobacco companies wouldn't do anything that was going to kill you so I figured ah, until they prove it to me . . . I didn't take it seriously. I'm being very honest with you. Maybe I didn't want to believe it."[8]

When doctors found a spot on her lung in 1981 and removed a tumor, Cipollone continued to smoke. Even after her right lung was removed a year later, Rose Cipollone smoked two to three cigarettes a day. In 1982, doctors found she had another cancerous tumor, but Cipollone did not stop smoking. Rose Cipollone finally quit smoking before her last operation in 1983.

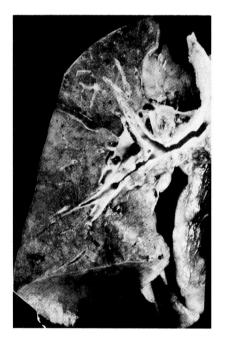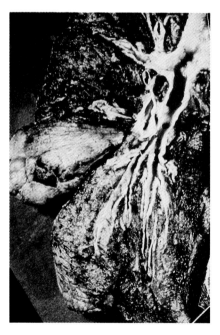

A healthy (nonsmoker's) lung is shown on the left. A diseased (smoker's) lung with emphysema is shown on the right.

Alan Naar, who represented the Liggett Group, cross-examined Rose Cipollone. At one point, he basically asked her the same question over and over. The question was about whether Cipollone had "specific recollection" of seeing each and every cigarette ad Marc Edell had marked for identification—a total of seventy-five ads.[9] "Oh, come on," she snapped. "Give me a break."[10]

Naar and other attorneys for the tobacco companies had every right to try to pin Cipollone down about which specific cigarette ads directly influenced her to smoke. It was necessary, because Cipollone claimed she was drawn into smoking at age sixteen by cigarette ads that made smoking seem glamorous. Remember, in the *Pritchard* case in 1954, the plaintiff could not prove that Liggett's Chesterfield ads had made him want to smoke (see Chapter 2).

Rose Cipollone said she first chose to smoke Chesterfield cigarettes because, "I thought it was glamorous. I used to see the ads of the pretty girls and movie stars. I thought it [smoking] was ladylike."[11] She testified she would buy her Chesterfield cigarettes three at a time, at a neighborhood candy store. Then, that same day, she would smoke all three cigarettes in the girl's bathroom at her high school. Within a year, Cipollone was smoking a pack a day.

Cipollone also claimed that the tobacco companies betrayed her by promoting that their brands of cigarettes were safe. "I know that through advertising," Cipollone said, "I was led to assume that [cigarettes] were safe and they wouldn't harm me." When pressed to name a specific brand or ad, she referred to L&M ads.[12]

As Rose Cipollone's cancer progressed, the physical effects on her became quite evident. Edell later recalled how she had worsened to "a skeleton covered with skin." He added, "If anyone ever saw it, they would never smoke."[13] Rose Cipollone died from cancer seven months after her deposition.

After Rose Cipollone's death in 1984, her husband, Antonio, filed an amended complaint on May 31, 1985. Antonio Cipollone, a retired cable splicer, sued on his own behalf and as the person in charge of his wife's estate. There would be several more years of legal battling between both parties before the *Cipollone* case came to trial. The complex case presented several important issues.

Warning Labels: Shield or Sword?

Early in the *Cipollone* case, two legal concepts were argued heatedly—strict liability and preemption. The Cipollones argued for strict liability. The tobacco companies argued for preemption.

Strict Liability. The concept of strict liability means that the seller is liable for a defective or dangerous product that unreasonably threatens a buyer's safety. This rule applies even though the seller has used "all possible care in the preparation and sale" of the product.[14] To win a case, the buyer who is harmed by the product must prove that the product was defective.

Preemption. The three tobacco companies claimed that the Federal Cigarette Labeling and Advertising Act of 1965 preempted state liability claims on their products. The preemption rule means that certain matters are of such a national importance (as opposed to a local importance), that federal laws take complete priority over state laws. In 1984, district court judge Lee Sarokin denied their motion (a request for a judge's action) to dismiss the *Cipollone* case on this basis of preemption.

Judge Sarokin concluded that Congress did not intend to prevent any debate over whether the federal warning labels adequately warned cigarette smokers of the health dangers. His ruling cleared the way for further information gathering and a trial.[15]

The tobacco makers appealed the ruling. The United States Court of Appeals for the Third Circuit heard their appeal. A federal circuit court has authority over states. There are thirteen courts of appeal in the federal court system. The Third Circuit covers the Virgin Islands and three states—New Jersey (where the *Cipollone* case was tried), Delaware, and Pennsylvania. These appeals courts do not conduct trials. Rather, they review written arguments and, in some cases, hear oral arguments by the parties' attorneys. This is to make sure that all procedures were followed, and

In 1984, district court judge Lee Sarokin denied the tobacco companies' legal request that the *Cipollone* case be dropped based on preemption.

that the judge made the correct legal ruling based on the facts presented.

On April 9, 1986, the Third Circuit overturned (reversed) Judge Sarokin's ruling. It found that the warning labels on cigarette packages did shield tobacco companies. In effect, the appeals court ruled that smokers could not later charge that they had not been warned of the health hazards. The ruling applied only to the area covered by the Third Circuit.

Antonio Cipollone then appealed the Third Circuit's ruling to the United States Supreme Court. On January 13, 1987, the Supreme Court "left standing" the ruling. It refused at that time to rule on the issue of legal immunity under federal law (see Chapter 6).

Despite this setback, Marc Edell, Antonio Cipollone's attorney, said that the case would still go to trial. But Edell would argue his case on other theories of liability under New Jersey law.[16]

Should Tobacco Documents Be Kept Secret or Released?

Another issue in the pretrial hearings was the release of private documents from the tobacco industry. After Cipollone's attorneys acquired these documents through the discovery process, the tobacco companies got a protective order to limit Cipollone's use of them at trial. Under this order, the documents could only be used for the trial and then they had to be returned or destroyed. The protective order allowed the tobacco companies to label any of the documents as secret. Cipollone's attorneys would need to show good cause in order to acquire any of these secret documents.

The issue here was whether the protective order placed unlawful limits on Cipollone's First Amendment freedoms. The First Amendment to the United States Constitution guarantees freedom of speech, among other things. Cipollone's attorneys wanted to be able to use the information in the documents for the *Cipollone* case and for other tobacco cases that they were prosecuting. They argued that the protective order violated Cipollone's and the public's right to publish the materials.

Cipollone wanted to release the documents to the public, as well. He believed the public had a right to know about the tobacco industry's activities. Some of the documents, he claimed, would reveal the tobacco industry's early knowledge of the risks of cigarette smoking. Other company memos would show the industry's plans to hide or play down the risks.

The tobacco companies claimed they had a constitutional right to keep their documents private. They argued that the use of the documents should remain limited to the *Cipollone* case. The release of certain secret documents, they claimed, could unfairly influence a jury against them.

The court battles over the release of the tobacco documents in the *Cipollone* case began in 1985 and lasted for several years. In 1985, Judge Sarokin overturned the protective order. Then in June 1987, an appeals court ruled that tobacco company papers *could* be disclosed to the public before their admission at the *Cipollone* trial.

The tobacco companies petitioned the United States Supreme Court for a review of the ruling of the appeals court. In December 1987, the Supreme Court denied their petition and "left standing" the June ruling by the Third Circuit Court of Appeals. In effect, the Supreme Court cleared the way for Marc Edell to disclose the documents and testimony obtained in pretrial discovery. The *Cipollone* case then returned to the federal court for trial.

Cipollone now had an advantage. Some of the information regarding the internal workings of the cigarette industry was quite damaging to the defense. The defendants, understandably, had argued to keep the information a secret until it was admitted as evidence in the *Cipollone* trial. That was because there were other liability lawsuits pending against the tobacco industry at that time.[17] Now plaintiffs in these other cases could also benefit from the documents, without spending additional time and money.

One of the newly released secret documents in question was a 1972 confidential report entitled "Motives and Incentives in Cigarette Smoking." The Philip Morris Research Center in Richmond, Virginia, prepared the report. It included the following frank and chilling explanation of the main use of a cigarette:

The cigarette should be conceived not as a product but as a package. The product is nicotine. . . . Think of the cigarette as a dispenser for a dose unit of nicotine. . . . Think of a puff of smoke as the vehicle of nicotine. . . . Smoke is beyond question the most optimized vehicle and the cigarette the most optimized dispenser of smoke.[18]

Despite the win for the Cipollones, the tobacco companies' delaying tactics also scored points. The tobacco companies had forced Marc Edell to go through a costly four-and-a-half-year legal process. Of the more than one hundred thousand internal documents he was able to obtain, Edell used about three hundred documents as evidence.[19]

1988 Civil Trial

Finally, after five years of legal maneuvering, the *Cipollone* civil trial got under way in 1988. Antonio Cipollone, Rose's husband, became the only plaintiff after her death in 1984. Edell's associate, Cynthia Walters, was in charge of Cipollone's medical witnesses. Alan Darnell (a partner at another New Jersey law firm) was also part of the team.

The lead attorneys for the defendants were: David K. Hardy and Robert E. Northrip, representing both Phillip Morris and Lorillard; and, Donald J. Cohn, representing Liggett. (Cohn, fifty-eight, was a twenty-three-year veteran of tobacco suits.)

During the trial, which lasted four and a half months,

Edell battled the tobacco companies over witnesses and additional evidence he wanted to use in the case. In particular, the tobacco companies sought to withhold evidence on the issue of nicotine addiction. They claimed that such information would unfairly hurt their case.

Finally, Rose Cipollone's testimony about her addiction to cigarettes was read aloud to the jurors. She had given this and other testimony at depositions prior to her death. Despite the fact that Rose Cipollone had died four years earlier, her testimony made her presence sharply felt at the trial.

"I felt like I had to have [cigarettes]. I couldn't give them up," she had explained. "It was very difficult for me. I craved them."[20]

The three tobacco companies, however, argued that Rose Cipollone freely chose to smoke. The defense based its arguments on the fact that she knew the risks of smoking but chose to smoke anyway.

Marc Edell addressed this issue directly in his opening statements at the trial on February 1, 1988. He said that Rose Cipollone made "a free choice and she chose to believe the defendants" (claim that smoking cigarettes was safe).[21]

The issues of nicotine addiction and free choice continue to pit smokers against tobacco companies and antismokers alike today. (See the *Castano* case in Chapter 7.)

Rose Cipollone's testimony also revealed that she had made an effort to smoke "safer" cigarettes. She changed brands several times over the course of her forty-year smoking habit. She switched from Chesterfields to L&M filter cigarettes in 1955. She recalled that in advertisements for L&M, "they were talking about the filter tip and it was milder, and a miracle [filter] that would keep that stuff inside the trap." By "that stuff" she meant "nicotine, that brown stuff."[22]

Cipollone switched to Virginia Slims in 1968 because "they were marvelous, so long and so attractive." She recalled the ad with the feminist message "You've come a long way, baby." In the early 1970s, she smoked Parliament cigarettes because "the filter was recessed."[23] Philip Morris, the maker of Parliament cigarettes, advertised the recessed filter as a superior filter because it did not touch a smoker's lips yet still trapped tar and nicotine.

Her final switch was to True cigarettes in 1974. Cipollone recalled the doctor saying "if you are going to smoke, smoke these." She also remembered seeing the ads for this brand that claimed "low tar and low nicotine, and I figured they were better."[24]

The defense attorneys also raised doubts about whether Rose Cipollone's smoking had caused her cancer. Their expert witnesses claimed she had a rare type of cancer.[25] Judge Sarokin, however, commented on the "irony" of the defense's position, because the tobacco companies also claimed "there is no type of cancer which has been proven to be caused by smoking."[26] (In other words, the fact that Rose Cipollone had a rare form of cancer, rather than a more common one, should not have mattered at all to the tobacco companies. They claimed that *her smoking could have caused no type of cancer.*)

Top-Secret "Safe" Cigarette Disclosed at Trial

Antonio Cipollone's attorneys claimed that the tobacco companies did not only market cigarettes that were defectively designed. They also failed to market a safer cigarette. At the trial, they presented evidence that such a cigarette was available as early as 1971.[27]

During his six-day testimony, Dr. Jeffrey Harris, the plaintiff's witness, claimed the cigarette makers knew of the scientific research on the safer cigarette. He revealed that such research was done by one of the defendants. The Liggett Company had conducted tests in their labs for many years on a safer, noncancer-causing cigarette. It was a top-secret project known as Project XA.

Dr. Harris knew about the secret research because he was a longtime Liggett researcher on Project XA. Project XA was dropped in 1987 because Liggett officials feared that this new "safe" cigarette would be an admission that they had made unsafe cigarettes before.[28]

Are Cigarettes Defective or of Social Value?

Generally, to decide whether or not a product is defective, its usefulness is compared with the risk of injury it poses to the public. This is known as the risk-utility analysis. The claim of risk-utility was another important issue argued at the trial.

Attorneys for the Cipollones argued that the risk-utility analysis should be applied in this case according to New Jersey's strict product liability law. (Product liability is the legal responsibility of sellers and makers.) Cigarettes, they argued, are dangerous and of little use. Therefore, they claimed, the court should find cigarettes to be defective, and hold the cigarette makers liable.[29]

The defendants argued that Congress itself had decided that the social usefulness of cigarettes "exceeds any costs associated with their use." They said that when Congress held hearings that led to the passage of the Federal Cigarette Labeling and Advertising Act of 1965, "prohibition of the sale of cigarettes was considered." However, "Congress opted instead to allow their sale," they argued, "and to prevent the destruction of the tobacco industry—as long as consumers were given the [warning labels]."[30]

Rose Cipollone had admitted in her deposition that she enjoyed smoking. But when asked to describe what she liked about smoking, she drew a blank. "I really don't know," she said. "All I know is that I had to smoke. I would panic if I didn't have any cigarettes around me."[31] (Today, we would associate this type of explanation with addiction to nicotine.)

In 1988, Judge Sarokin ruled that the New Jersey Product Liability Act (adopted in 1987) overrode Cipollone's defective product claim. This state law held that makers of drugs, drug devices, food, and food additives must use FDA-approved warnings or instructions on their products. These product warnings prevented liability claims.[32] Judge Sarokin also threw out the "risk-utility" claim against all three cigarette makers.

Final Arguments

On June 1, 1988, the defense attorneys began their closing statements. Donald Cohn, representing Liggett, emphasized the theme of personal choice to the jury. In his description of Rose Cipollone, he said:

> [Rose] was intelligent. She was strong-minded. She was well read. She had a mind of her own. She was used to making decisions for herself and her family. This is a woman who was in control of her life. She wanted to do what she wanted to do. She wanted to smoke. She smoked.[33]

Later, in the jury room, the jurors would also focus on Rose Cipollone's character. Most of the jurors agreed with the defense that she was strong-minded, but they were more sympathetic toward her husband.[34]

Defense attorney Robert Northrip, representing Lorillard, focused his closing statements on Rose Cipollone's type of cancer. Then, Peter Bleakely, representing Philip Morris, said the tobacco industry did not misrepresent the risks of smoking. It merely stated its "opinion" that there was no direct proof that smoking caused cancer.[35]

In final arguments for the plaintiff, Marc Edell blasted

the tobacco industry in general, and Liggett, Philip Morris, and Lorillard in particular. "What you have seen in this case," he said, "is an evil-minded conspiracy" by the tobacco companies to make money and to deceive the public.[36]

Landmark Jury Award

After a four-and-a-half-month trial, Judge Sarokin gave a final address to the jury. The seventy-two-page charge was awesome. It included a summary of the case and a list of instructions about the rules of law that apply to the various issues. The jurors were also given a list of twenty written questions they would have to answer in order to reach a verdict. With that, the difficult task of sorting out the complex issues in the case became immediately apparent to the jurors.

The six-member jury was made up of three men and three women. Three jurors were non-smokers, two were ex-smokers, and one was a smoker. They had been picked from among the 233 potential jurors who had filled out a question form in January 1988. The jury selection process took eight days.

On June 7, 1988, the jury began to discuss the issues of the *Cipollone* case and consider the judge's list of questions. But first, the jurors voted to see where each of them stood on the issue of Rose Cipollone's type of cancer. During the trial, medical witnesses for the defense had raised doubts in the jurors' minds about whether cigarette smoking caused

Cipollone's type of cancer. The jurors voted 5 to 1 in favor of the defense witnesses that claimed her cancer was a rare form, and was not caused by smoking. "If we all thought [Rose Cipollone's cancer] wasn't caused by smoking," one juror said later, "we could have stopped [our discussion] right there."[37] But since they were also bound by the questions on the verdict form (and Judge Sarokin had not allowed this issue to be listed there), the jurors turned their attention to the list of questions.

Keep in mind that the jury had four claims to consider against Liggett. These claims were fraud, conspiracy, failure to warn, and express warranty. The jurors had only two claims to consider against both Philip Morris and Lorillard. These claims were fraud and conspiracy. The claims of failure to warn and express warning were dropped against these two tobacco companies as a result of the court's rulings two months earlier. (Rose Cipollone had smoked two Philip Morris products after 1966—Virginia Slims and Parliaments. She had smoked one Lorillard product after 1966—True cigarettes.)

After five and a half days, the jurors returned their verdict on June 13, 1988. The jury issued three judgments: [38]

- They entered a judgment "in favor of plaintiff Antonio Cipollone and against defendant Liggett, Inc., in the amount of $400,000.00."

- They entered a judgment of "no cause of action in favor of Philip Morris and against plaintiff Antonio Cipollone."

- They entered a judgment of "no cause of action be entered in favor of Lorillard, Inc., and against Antonio Cipollone."

"No cause of action" is the equivalent of "not guilty" in a criminal case. The jury found that Cipollone had *not* proven his case against Philip Morris and Lorillard. The jury found these two tobacco companies not guilty. The jurors believed that these post-1966 claims of conspiracy and fraud against them (when warning labels on cigarette packages were in effect) were not valid.

The jurors had found Liggett guilty. But how did the jurors vote on each of the four claims against Liggett?

- *Fraudulent misrepresentation.* The jury found that Cipollone had *not* proven that Liggett had misled its customers before 1966 on the risks of smoking.

- *Conspiracy.* The jury also *rejected* the claim that Liggett conspired to defraud the public by hiding the dangers of smoking.

- *Failure to warn.* The jury found that Liggett, before 1966, *had* failed to warn Rose Cipollone and other smokers of the known health risks of smoking.

The jury, however, did not award any money damages to Rose Cipollone's estate for her pain and suffering. It found

Antonio Cipollone (left) talks with the press, as lawyer Mark Edell (right) looks on during a press conference the day after the victory in court.

that she had "voluntarily and unreasonably encountered a known danger by smoking cigarettes." The jury also found that Rose Cipollone was 80 percent responsible for her own injuries.[39] Under New Jersey law, it meant that her estate could not receive any money.[40]

In New Jersey, jurors are allowed to award money by looking at the degree to which the injured party contributed to his or her own injury. If a jury finds that the person suing is 60 percent or more responsible, then he or she cannot receive any money from the defendants. That is because the person is more responsible than the defendants.

- *Breach of express warranty.* The jury found that Liggett *had* made false pledges in their advertising before 1966 that their cigarettes were not harmful. (Remember, Rose Cipollone had smoked two Liggett products before 1966—Chesterfields, from 1942 to 1955, and L&Ms, from 1955 to 1968.) However, the jury also decided that Liggett was *not* liable for any claims after 1966, when the federal warning labels were in effect.

For the verdict against Liggett on the express warranty claim (in which damages *were* recoverable), however, the jury awarded $400,000 in damages to Rose Cipollone's widower, Antonio. The Liggett Group was ordered to pay the damages as compensation for Antonio Cipollone's losses.

Interviews with some of the jurors after the trial revealed that four of the jurors were pro-defense.[41] Some of the jurors later said they had compromised on the $400,000 award at the urging of two other jurors. "We thought it was a small amount [to Liggett] and not too small to Mr. Cipollone," explained a juror. "It would more or less get across the message." The message for Liggett and other tobacco companies was that they should have said that their cigarettes could be harmful.[42]

Why was the $400,000 damage award a landmark award? It was not necessarily because of the large amount of money (by historical standards) awarded to Antonio Cipollone. It was a landmark award because it was the nation's *first* damage award judgment in a smoking-related death case. The tobacco industry had been involved in over three hundred liability lawsuits since 1954. Until the *Cipollone* case, however, the tobacco industry had never lost a liability lawsuit.[43]

The three tobacco companies had reportedly spent more than $50 million to defend themselves in the *Cipollone* case up to that point. Marc Edell's law firm had spent nearly $4 million.[44]

$400,000 Judgment Award Overturned

Antonio Cipollone and the three tobacco companies appealed the verdict. Cipollone wanted additional damages for pre-judgment interest, medical costs, and legal fees. He also wanted money damages awarded to his late wife's estate. Liggett wanted the $400,000 damage award completely overturned.

On January 5, 1990, the Court of Appeals for the Third Circuit ruled as follows:

- Judge Sarokin should have informed the jury to consider Rose Cipollone's post-1965 smoking habit only when considering money to be awarded—and not the extent of her responsibility. Therefore, the appeals court threw out the $400,000 judgment awarded to Antonio Cipollone.

- Post-1965 claims were prohibited by the Labeling Act of 1965.

- Liggett could be held liable for failure to warn claims before the 1965 law.

- Liggett, Philip Morris, and Lorillard could be held liable for claims of express warranty and risk utility.

- It ordered a new trial.

Antonio Cipollone died at age sixty-six of heart failure on January 10, 1990. He had continued the legal battle after his wife's death at age fifty-eight of lung cancer in 1984. The Cipollones' son, Thomas, waged the next and final battle in the United States Supreme Court.

4

The Arguments for Cipollone

How does a court case reach the United States Supreme Court? There are several routes, but the most common way a case makes it to the Supreme Court is by an order called a writ of *certiorari*. The Latin term *certiorari* means, "to be informed of." When a case has gone through state court to the highest state court or through the federal district and appeals courts, it may be eligible for a hearing by the United States Supreme Court. However, since many thousands of lawsuits are filed in federal and state courts every year, the United States Supreme Court must have special standards and a method for selecting the cases it will decide. The cases the Supreme Court agrees to hear generally have strong national significance or involve a dispute over a constitutional issue.[1]

How the Supreme Court Works

Being heard by the United States Supreme Court is a two-step process. First, a party must ask the Court to hear its case. The party files a writ of *certiorari*, explaining the reasons the case should be heard. The Supreme Court grants fewer than 2 percent of the annual petitions for writ of *certiorari*.[2] Then, if the Court "grants *certiorari*" and agrees to hear the case, it orders the lower court to send the record of the case to the Supreme Court. Both parties file briefs, or written legal arguments. The parties are scheduled for oral arguments before the nine Justices. The Supreme Court has final authority over all other judicial rulings.

Cipollone Case Reaches the Supreme Court

On March 25, 1991, the United States Supreme Court responded to a petition by the Cipollone family and agreed to hear the case. By that time, the *Cipollone* case had been in the lower courts for over eight years.

The Court agreed to rule on smokers' legal rights against cigarette makers who claimed legal immunity, or protection, under the federal warning labels. The Court would interpret the 1965 Labeling Act and the 1969 amendment to this act. The main legal issue was whether either or both acts protect the cigarette companies from state liability claims. It was the same issue that the Supreme Court had refused to consider in 1987.

What caused the Court to change its mind? In 1991,

Procedural Steps of *Cipollone* v. *Liggett* Through the Court System

United States Federal District Court (Newark, New Jersey)

August 1, 1983—Rose and Antonio Cipollone file their first complaint.

May 31, 1985—First amended complaint filed by Antonio Cipollone after his wife's death.

June 13, 1988—Trial jury awarded $400,000 to Antonio Cipollone; No money awarded to Rose Cipollone's estate.

1988—Second amended complaint filed by Antonio Cipollone.

1990—Third amended complaint filed by Tom Cipollone after his father's death.

United States Third Circuit Court of Appeals

April 9, 1986—Pretrial ruling; 1965 Labeling Act preempted post-1965 damage claims.

January 5, 1990—$400,000 jury award overturned; labeling law ruled a tobacco industry shield.

Supreme Court of the United States

December 1987—Antonio Cipollone's petition for writ of *certiorari* of 1986 third circuit ruling denied.

January 13, 1991—Tom Cipollone's petition for writ of *certiorari* of 1990 third circuit ruling granted.

October 8, 1991—Case argued.

January 13, 1992—Case reargued.

June 24, 1992—Case decided.

both the Cipollone family and Liggett Group, Inc., had asked the Supreme Court to step in.[3] Another strong reason for the Court's change of mind was the fact that there were about forty-five similar lawsuits against the tobacco industry in lower courts across the country in 1991. Until then, these courts had been split over the immunity issue regarding the federal warning labels. Generally, the federal courts ruled in favor of the tobacco companies while several state courts ruled in favor of the smokers.[4]

In 1990, for example, the New Jersey Supreme Court ruled in favor of the plaintiff in *Dewey* v. *R.J. Reynolds Tobacco Co.* (a case similar to *Cipollone*). This court said the 1965 Federal Cigarette Labeling Act did not override the tobacco companies' liability of state law claims after 1965.[5] However, because the *Cipollone* civil liability case was tried in a federal court, this ruling could not apply to it.

Claims Against Liggett Group, Inc.

The Cipollones' son, Thomas, was the petitioner. A petitioner is a person who files a petition with the Supreme Court. Liggett Group, Inc., was the respondent in this case. A respondent is the opposing party. Tom Cipollone made four common-law claims against the cigarette companies, based on the issues presented to the trial court. Common law is a set of rules and principles that govern all people and property. It is established only by usage and custom. The four claims were:

- *Failure to Warn*: Cigarette companies were "negligent in the manner [that] they tested, researched, sold, promoted, and advertised" their cigarettes. Also, respondents failed to provide "adequate warnings of the health consequences of cigarette smoking."

- *Breach of Express Warranty*: Cigarette companies failed to honor the promises they made in their cigarette advertisements.

- *Fraudulent Misrepresentation*: Cigarette companies canceled out the effect of the federal warning labels through their advertising.

- *Conspiracy to Defraud*: Cigarette companies misrepresented or concealed the facts concerning the health hazards of smoking.[6]

1991 Briefs for Cipollone

Attorneys for Tom Cipollone filed a brief with the Supreme Court. They argued these four basic points:[7]

- Congress did not clearly intend to override Cipollone's common law claims.

- Congress did not clearly intend to override Cipollone's common law claims by its attempts to regulate the tobacco industry.

- Cipollone's common law claims do not actually conflict with the Labeling Act of 1965.

- Congress did not override Cipollone's claims of intentional wrongful acts by the cigarette companies.

69

Cipollone's request for the Court's action came at the end of this written argument. He asked the Supreme Court to reverse the decision of the United States Court of Appeals for the Third Circuit and to send the case back to the trial court "for further proceedings."[8] (In 1986, the Third Circuit had overturned the trial judge's ruling. It had found that the warning labels did shield the tobacco companies.)

Other briefs, known as "friends of the court" were filed in support of Cipollone. They included former surgeons general, health organizations, and twelve states, including New Jersey. The American Medical Association (AMA), for example, attacked the tobacco companies' position that Congress intended to shield them. The AMA made the point that Congress had passed many federal laws that regulated other areas of the public's safety, including food, drugs, air, and water.[9]

Oral Arguments

The Supreme Court holds its sessions from October through June each year. The Justices ask questions during oral arguments. A limited number of seats are available to the public to witness these proceedings.

On October 8, 1991, the Supreme Court heard oral arguments in the *Cipollone* case. Marc Edell presented his arguments before the Court regarding the preemption issues of the two federal labeling laws. He argued that it was not Congress' intent to prevent injured smokers from suing tobacco companies in a state court. Rather, the Cigarette Labeling and Advertising Act of 1965 was meant to stop states from making their own such regulations.[10]

Edell also made the argument that Congress amended the 1965 Act in 1969 because the preemption that applied to warning labels in advertisements "was to expire on July 1, 1969." Congress did not act because the cigarette companies needed protection from pending lawsuits.[11]

Only eight of the nine Supreme Court Justices heard the *Cipollone* case in early October 1991. Those eight Justices were: Chief Justice William Rehnquist, Justices Byron R. White, Harry A. Blackmun, John Paul Stevens, Sandra Day O'Connor, Antonin Scalia, Anthony M. Kennedy, and David H. Souter.

Clarence Thomas, who was to replace the retired Justice Thurgood Marshall, had not yet been confirmed. Marshall retired on June 27, 1991. Thomas was sworn in as the ninth Justice on November 1, 1991. The Court ordered that the *Cipollone* case be re-argued in January 1992 but gave no formal reason for doing so.

On January 13, 1992, the full Court revisited the *Cipollone* case. The Court included the newly confirmed ninth Justice, Clarence Thomas, who was a cigar smoker. The other two smokers on the Court were Scalia and Rehnquist.[12]

This time, Laurence Tribe replaced Marc Edell as Tom Cipollone's lawyer. Tribe was a Harvard law professor and a

When the Supreme Court revisited the *Cipollone* case in 1992, Laurence Tribe (shown here) replaced Marc Edell as Tom Cipollone's attorney.

well-respected constitutional lawyer. Edell made the difficult decision to step aside because "a new voice, a new perspective was probably the best way to go."[13]

Laurence Tribe had appeared before the Court nineteen times and had won all five preemption cases that he had argued. He took this case free of charge because, "Apart from being legally right, I think the case is of great social importance, and it's challenging."[14]

Tribe argued that the 1965 Labeling Act was not intended as an "ironclad guarantee as far as the 50 states are concerned that the cigarette companies can do no wrong."[15]

5

The Arguments for Liggett Group, Inc.

The respondents (what the defendants are called at the Supreme Court level) in the *Cipollone* case were Liggett Group, Inc., Philip Morris, and Loews Corporation (the parent company of Lorillard). H. Bartow Farr, III, filed a written argument for the three tobacco companies. Later, he presented an oral argument before the United States Supreme Court. Charles Wall, another attorney, also represented the tobacco companies.

1991 Briefs for Tobacco Companies

Farr made the following main points in his written argument:[1]

- The 1965 Labeling Act bars state laws related to smoking and health. So, tobacco companies cannot be held responsible for failing to use additional health warnings other than the federal warning labels on cigarette packages.

- A state lawsuit cannot be used as a means of controlling the tobacco industry. This interferes with Congress's own design in the form of the 1965 Labeling Act.

Farr gave two main reasons in support of his preemption claim. He wrote that Congress intended that the federal government—not the states—should make the final decisions "about what the cigarette companies must or must not say." He also stated that Congress did not want the states to make any restrictions that would "upset the balance of . . . national interest."[2]

Farr ended his written argument with a request for the Court's action. He asked the Supreme Court to affirm, or uphold, the judgment of the United States Court of Appeals for the Third Circuit.[3]

Others in support of the tobacco companies filed separate briefs. The groups included the National Association of Manufacturers, the Association of National Advertisers, and the Product Liability Advisory Council.

The National Association of Manufacturers (NAM) wrote that the 1965 Labeling Act also was intended to address public health concerns, but that was not its only purpose. NAM, like Farr, argued that the interests of the national economy and the "competing claims of interstate

Charles Wall, representing the tobacco companies, is seen outside the Supreme Court building in Washington, D.C., where the *Cipollone* case was heard.

commerce" also figured prominently in the wording of the Labeling Act. It also believed that Congress may have created some of the confusion in the preemption issue with the actual wording of the Labeling Act. Its position was that the Supreme Court needed to rule on what Congress intended in this act.[4]

The Association of National Advertisers stressed to the Court the importance of Congress's role—to inform the public of health hazards, while protecting businesses and the companies' right to conduct business without unnecessary regulations.[5]

Oral Arguments

Liggett Group, Inc., used the federal preemption theory to discredit Cipollone's claims before the Supreme Court. It was the same defense strategy the cigarette companies had argued at the federal trial. This time the stakes were higher. If they were successful before the Supreme Court, the cigarette companies would not only be free of liability in the *Cipollone* case but also of all smokers' liability claims in state court cases throughout the nation.[6] (The ruling of the Supreme Court would overpower any and all state rulings that were already in effect.)

Farr argued that the Federal Cigarette Labeling and Advertising Act of 1965 exempts, or excuses, the tobacco industry from state regulation. He claimed that the Public Health Cigarette Smoking Act of 1969 protects cigarette makers from any liability "based on their conduct after 1965."[7]

Farr also argued that Congress had set forth a "national standard of conduct" for tobacco companies when it enacted the labeling laws. To achieve this, he argued, Congress meant to stop states from enforcing their own regulations in state courts.[8]

The preemption defense also raised the issue of states' rights in the *Cipollone* case. Here the issue concerned whether or not the federal government's regulations—namely, the warning labels—override liability lawsuits against the tobacco industry in state courts.[9]

Now it was up to the Supreme Court to decide the issue of preemption. Would the Court favor Cipollone or the tobacco companies? Or, would it find differently altogether?

6

The Decision

The full Supreme Court in 1992 consisted of the following nine members: Chief Justice William H. Rehnquist, Justice Byron R. White, Justice John Paul Stevens, Justice Harry A. Blackmun, Justice Sandra Day O'Connor, Justice Antonin Scalia, Justice Anthony M. Kennedy, Justice David H. Souter, and Justice Clarence Thomas.

The Supreme Court Justices had already heard oral arguments. They had read written briefs from both sides of the *Cipollone* case under their review from a lower court. The Justices then met in conference to discuss the case.

In practice, the Chief Justice, who presides over the conference, gives his or her views first. Next, the eight Associate Justices take turns, according to seniority, in presenting their views. Then a vote is taken. This time, the Justices with the least seniority vote first. Finally, the senior Justice in the majority assigns the writing of opinions. An opinion is a written explanation of the Court's decision. All of these proceedings take place in private.[1]

Supreme Court's Splintered Decision

On June 24, 1992, the Supreme Court of the United States issued its decision in the *Cipollone* case. The long-awaited decision was split. This is known as a plurality opinion. It is an opinion in which more Justices joined than not, but there

The members of the Supreme Court in 1992 were (standing left to right): Justice David Souter, Justice Antonin Scalia, Justice Anthony Kennedy, and Justice Clarence Thomas; (sitting left to right): Justice John Paul Stevens, Justice Byron White, Chief Justice William Rehnquist, Justice Harry Blackmun, and Justice Sandra Day O'Connor.

is no clear majority. Regardless, this opinion becomes the "law of the land."

At the heart of the decision, of course, were the preemption issues of the two federal warning label laws—the Cigarette Labeling and Advertising Act (1965) and the Public Health Cigarette Smoking Act (1969). Did these federal laws override claims based on state law?

Justice Stevens wrote that the preemption status of the federal government is provided in Article VI of the U.S. Constitution. It states, in part, that the laws of the United States "shall be the supreme Law of the Land; . . . anything in the Constitution or Laws of any state to the Contrary notwithstanding." This so-called Supremacy Clause means that federal laws preempt, or override, state laws.

The issue of federal preemption was first tested in the landmark 1819 case *McCulloch* v. *Maryland.* The Supreme Court had ruled that any state law that conflicts with federal law is "without effect."[2] In other words, if a federal law and a state law conflict, the federal law always wins.

To decide the preemption issues in the *Cipollone* case, the Justices needed to interpret Congress' intent when drafting these labeling laws. The main point was whether Congress intended to protect cigarette makers from state liability claims as long as these companies used federal warning labels on their products and in their advertising. Among other things, the Justices relied on the phrasing of the preemption clause (Section 5) in each Act, statements in congressional records, and the historical context of the clause.[3]

The nine Justices, however, were divided on the issues of preemption. Four opinions were issued, but only one of these opinions was the opinion of the Court.

Opinion of the Court

Justice Stevens wrote the opinion of the Court with respect to Parts I, II, III, and IV. He was joined by Chief Justice Rehnquist and Justices White, Blackmun, O'Connor, Kennedy, and Souter. This opinion dealt mostly with Section 5 of the 1965 Act. They concluded that this section *does not* prevent lawsuits for claims under state law. Justice Stevens wrote that Section 5 of this act overrides only warnings by state law on cigarette labels or in advertisements. He reasoned that Congress meant only to prevent states from adding many different kinds of regulations. Therefore, the federal warning itself does not rule out additional legal duties of cigarette makers required by a state.[4]

The Justices, however, had varying opinions that dealt with the preemption status of Section 5 of the 1969 Act. However, since there was no majority opinion, no official Court opinion was issued on this aspect of the case.

By removing some types of lawsuits, Justice Blackmun reasoned, the Court was removing a "critical component of the states' traditional ability to protect the health and safety of their citizens." He also thought that the lower courts would have difficulty carrying out the Supreme Court's decision.[5]

Responses to the Court's Decision

How did Tom Cipollone and his supporters respond to the Court's splintered decision? They claimed victory. For Tom Cipollone, the Court's decision was a family concern. The decision "has special significance to me in memory of my parents and the long and committed battle they fought as their last acts in life," he said.[6]

"My mother, Rose Cipollone, in particular," Tom continued, "wanted to make the public aware of her pain and anguish caused by her use of cigarettes and hoped by bringing this lawsuit she might prevent others from smoking."[7]

Marc Edell said the decision meant that the tobacco industry "remains at risk" for its conduct both before and after 1965.[8]

Laurence Tribe said, "Now that the court has made it possible to sue the tobacco industry and hold it accountable for its deceptive practices, it will be really quite a new day for these lawsuits. They will have a meaningful day in court."[9]

The health community also supported the Court's ruling. Three leading health organizations (the American Cancer Society, the American Lung Association, and the American Heart Association) issued a joint statement. They said that the Court's decision "denies tobacco manufacturers the license they sought to lie and mislead the American public about their deadly products."[10]

The tobacco companies claimed victory, too. Steve Parrish, general counsel for Philip Morris said, "This opinion is not going to lead to a flood of new cases being filed."[11]

James Kearney, a Liggett lawyer, said, "For the last 38 years, tobacco companies have been winning these cases because juries have consistently rejected claims that smokers were misled about health risks." On the future success of smokers' cases, Kearney added, "they still won't be able to find a jury that will agree with those claims."[12]

What effect would the Court's ruling have on the state of New Jersey's own product liability law? Edward Slaughter, Jr., a New Jersey plaintiff's attorney, pointed out that the state's product liability law of 1987 protects companies from "failure to warn" lawsuits if they use warnings or instructions on their products. Since this law "really hasn't been changed," he said, the impact of the Supreme Court's ruling in the *Cipollone* case would not make "a lot of difference one way or the other."[13]

In the Final Analysis

Was the Supreme Court's decision in the *Cipollone* case a closed door or a window of opportunity for people to sue tobacco makers? The Court's splintered decision meant that the Justices did not unanimously agree on one definitive interpretation of the preemption clauses in both the 1965 and 1969 acts. The fact that all parties concerned with the Court's decision claimed victory showed that perhaps the final battle was yet to be decided.

In the final analysis, the Supreme Court did not decide the issue of preemption once and for all. Rather, it sent the *Cipollone* case back to the lower court for retrial, though on more narrow claims.

Cipollone Suit Dropped

After the Supreme Court ruling, it was expected that Tom Cipollone would continue his legal battle in a lower court. However, the Cipollone suit was never retried. In 1992, the suit was dropped, with the permission of the Cipollone family.

Marc Edell and his law firm wanted the case dismissed because of the huge legal expenses it had cost them. The law firm said it spent $5 million in lawyers' time and another $1.2 million in out-of-pocket expenses prosecuting the Cipollone case.[14] In comparison, the three tobacco companies spent over $50 million for their defense.[15]

On November 5, 1992, Judge Dickinson R. Debevoise (who replaced Judge Sarokin) of the United States District Court dismissed the *Cipollone* case "with prejudice."[16] This meant that the case could not be reopened later. However, as many predicted, the effects of this case have been felt through the years.

7

Where We Stand Today

The Supreme Court decision in the *Cipollone* case set new standards for preemption in tobacco cases that followed. Who would benefit? "The tobacco litigation now has no end," Marc Edell said of the Court's decision. "It has a long tail."[1] He was right. Important legal cases rode on the "tail" of the *Cipollone* case.

Some legal gains were the result of creative strategies and legal arguments by the states. Other gains were due to the collective legal strength and financial clout of smokers who sued as groups. Still other gains came from former employees of tobacco companies who revealed hidden truths of the tobacco industry's deceptive policies and practices. Without this information, smokers (like those in earlier lawsuits) would have a difficult time proving their claims of fraudulent misrepresentation and conspiracy by the tobacco makers in court. When all the "smoke" finally cleared, the tobacco industry was undeniably damaged financially and publicly and was vulnerable to federal regulation.

Class-Action Lawsuits

Castano v. *American Tobacco Co.* was filed in New Orleans, Louisiana, in March 1994. It was one of the largest class-action suits brought by nicotine-addicted smokers against the tobacco industry. A class-action suit is brought by a group of people with common complaints against a person or persons. There is a single trial. Peter Castano, whose name was used to represent the numerous plaintiffs, was a Louisiana attorney who died of lung cancer.

The *Castano* case involved sixty-five law firms from various states. The plaintiffs' plan was to pool the financial and legal resources necessary to support a legal battle against the tobacco companies. Their legal strategy was to focus on nicotine addiction and the tobacco industry's alleged lies about it.

As in the *Cipollone* case, the *Castano* case pitted the tobacco industry's "free-choice" argument against the smokers' addiction argument.[2] However, the plaintiffs in this case claimed, among other things, that tobacco companies manipulated the amounts of nicotine in their products in order to addict smokers.

Two years later, however, an appeals court disqualified the *Castano* case. The court ruled that there were too many plaintiffs and too many states involved.[3] Lawyers for the *Castano* plaintiffs then began filing class-action suits in individual states.

A $200 billion class-action tobacco suit was filed in Miami, Florida, in 1994. Howard Engle and eight other lead plaintiffs sued on behalf of approximately five hundred thousand smokers who were ill. *Engle* v. *R.J. Reynolds Tobacco Co.* was the first tobacco class-action suit of its kind to go to trial.[4]

The smokers claimed that R.J. Reynolds and four other tobacco companies, as well as the Tobacco Institute, knew about the hazards of smoking but hid that information from the public. The tobacco companies argued that it was the smokers' choice to smoke and their responsibility.

In July 1999, the *Engle* jury found the five tobacco companies and the Tobacco Institute liable for the plaintiffs' smoking-related illnesses. In April 2000, it ordered them to pay $12.7 million as compensation for the ill smokers. Three months later, the jury ordered them to pay a total of over $144 billion as punishment for their misconduct. Of this total, each tobacco company was ordered to pay the following: more than $74 billion for Philip Morris, more than $35 billion for R.J. Reynolds, $16 billion for Brown & Williamson, $16 billion for Lorillard, and $790 million for Liggett.

The tobacco industry is appealing the decision. Because Florida law does not allow damage awards that could put a company out of business, some experts say that the amount of damages will be reduced. Attorneys for the tobacco companies argued that the steep penalties would bankrupt the industry. Attorneys for the smokers disagreed.

In 1994, the state of Mississippi sued the tobacco industry. It became the first state to try to win back Medicaid costs (state health care money awarded to the "medically needy") for smoking-related illnesses. It was a bold strategy for Attorney General Mike Moore and attorney Dick Scruggs of Mississippi. Other states would soon follow Mississippi's example. Mississippi, along with Florida, Texas, and Minnesota, settled their suits with Philip Morris, R.J. Reynolds, and Lorillard for $40 billion.

This new legal strategy ultimately brought the tobacco industry to the bargaining table. In 1999, the attorneys general of the remaining forty-six states accepted a $206 billion settlement with the cigarette companies.

Secondhand Smoke

Secondhand smoke is exposure to tobacco smoke by non-smokers. (It is also known as environmental tobacco smoke or passive smoke.) It contains the same toxic chemicals that a smoker inhales. These toxic agents can cause cancer.

Exposure to secondhand smoke is not a new health issue. In 1986, the Surgeon General reported that secondhand smoke caused lung cancer. According to the Environmental Protection Agency (EPA) in 1993, secondhand smoke was the cause of about three thousand deaths from lung cancer each year.[5] It also causes respiratory diseases such as emphysema and asthma.

The issue of the rights of nonsmokers who are subjected to cigarette smoke has been argued successfully in a court of law. In 1997, after a four-month trial, four major tobacco companies settled out of court with flight attendants who had filed a $5 billion class-action lawsuit against them in the *Broin* case in Florida. The flight attendants (totaling about sixty thousand) had claimed that their health was damaged as a result of exposure to secondhand smoke on airlines. (Until 1990, smoking had been allowed on many domestic airline flights.)

Brown & Williamson, Philip Morris, R.J. Reynolds, and Lorillard agreed to a $349 million settlement with the flight attendants. Of this total amount, $300 million would go to fund a research center for smoking-related diseases. The remaining $49 million would go to the attorneys for legal fees. However, as part of the agreement, the flight attendants received no money damages. Also, the four tobacco companies did not have to admit that secondhand smoke was a health risk to nonsmokers. The proposed settlement was appealed by some flight attendants who opposed the terms of the settlement. Two years later, they dropped their appeal. The objectors settled instead for a small percentage of the $49 million payment to the lead attorneys who represented the flight attendants in the lawsuit.

Individual Smokers Sue

In the aftermath of this national class-action settlement, it was expected that lawsuits brought by individual smokers or their survivors against the tobacco industry would dwindle. Lawsuits that were brought by individual smokers fared surprisingly well.

In 1996, a Florida state circuit court jury awarded Grady Carter $750,000. The loser was Brown & Williamson. This was only the second financial judgment ever against a tobacco company for smoking liability. The *Cipollone* federal case has been the first. From 1954 to 1996, there were over one thousand cases brought against the tobacco industry.[6]

Carter, who smoked Lucky Strikes, contracted lung cancer. He claimed that Lucky Strikes cigarettes were a defective product and that the maker of this brand of cigarettes, Brown & Williamson, was negligent for failing to warn consumers. The jury agreed. One juror said that the damaging Brown & Williamson documents (released in 1994) had affected the jury's decision.[7]

However, in 1998 a Florida appeals court reversed the *Carter* decision because of a legal time limit. The court found that Carter had waited too long to file a lawsuit. Under Florida law, there is a four-year time limit. Carter filed suit four years and six days from the time he learned he had lung cancer in 1991. He was six days too late.

In 1997, a Florida jury in *Raulerson* v. *R.J. Reynolds Tobacco* failed to find R.J. Reynolds negligent. Connor had smoked the company's Winston and Salem brands of cigarettes. The family of Jean Connor blamed the tobacco company for her lung cancer and subsequent death. Dana Raulerson, Connor's sister, represented Connor's estate in the lawsuit.

Although the *Raulerson* jury had decided that the tobacco maker's cigarettes were not overly dangerous and did not cause Connor's cancer, R.J. Reynolds responded to the public's increasing health concerns over cigarettes three years later. The company made a bold announcement about a "safer" cigarette it had been marketing in several cities since 1996, one year before the *Raulerson* trial. The tobacco company claimed publicly for the first time that its Eclipse brand was safer than other cigarettes, including other brands the company made, because it reduced smoke. The reduced smoke in Eclipse cigarettes was achieved by heating instead of burning the tobacco. However, critics said that these "safer" cigarettes were just as dangerous as the old ones, because the new ones contain glass fibers. R.J. Reynolds planned to continue to test-market Eclipse cigarettes in various cities.

In February 1999, a state court jury in San Francisco, California, awarded $51.5 million to Patricia Henley. Henley, who had lung cancer, was a longtime smoker of Marlboro cigarettes. The judge later reduced the damage award to $26.5 million. He also denied a request by Philip Morris, the maker of Marlboro cigarettes, for a new trial.

Philip Morris, the largest tobacco company in the world, had a net worth of over $3.4 billion. The judge, however, said the reduced award was "large by any standard" and provided "substantial discomfort" to the tobacco company.[8]

One month later, another Marlboro smoker who contracted lung cancer hit Philip Morris with an even larger judgment. A jury in Portland, Oregon, awarded $81 million to the family of the deceased smoker, Jesse Williams. The damage award for an individual smoker was the largest ever against a tobacco company. In May 1999, a judge reduced the award to $33.5 million. However, this victory should be viewed with caution because no smoking liability verdict to date has ever survived on appeal.[9]

Another San Francisco jury made news in March 2000 in *Whiteley* v. *Raybestos-Manhattan* when it voted in favor of dying smoker Leslie Whiteley, despite the fact that she was aware of the health risks when she started smoking. The verdict was the first of its kind in the nation. The jury was persuaded by evidence that tobacco makers had hidden from the public for years, and then challenged at trial. The tobacco industry's private documents showed that cigarette makers knew of tobacco's health risks in the 1950s.

After a two-month trial, the jury ordered the tobacco makers to pay Whiteley a total of $21.7 million. The verdict is being appealed.

Whistle-Blowers Inform on Tobacco Industry

A whistle-blower is a person who reveals secret information or informs on someone else. Depending on which side of the issue you are on, he or she can be characterized as a traitor or a hero.

Several whistle-blowers, people who spoke out against the tobacco companies, disclosed valuable inside information to government officials and, ultimately, to the public. The information supported the claims of many that had said that the tobacco industry had misled the public about the dangers of cigarette smoking.

One whistle-blower mentioned earlier was Dr. Jeffrey Harris. Harris had been a researcher for Liggett. He later testified for Antonio Cipollone at the federal trial. Dr. Harris revealed that Liggett had developed a safer cigarette in the early 1970s. He stated that the project was later discarded because Liggett feared lawsuits. The company reasoned that an announcement of a safer cigarette would be seen as an admission that its cigarettes already on the market were unsafe. Instead, Liggett stood firm by its long-held claim that its cigarettes were safe.

Another notable whistle-blower was William Farone. On April 14, 1994, Farone watched a televised congressional hearing with great interest. The seven executives of the nation's biggest tobacco companies were testifying before the House Energy and Commerce subcommittee. Under oath, each man made startling denials:

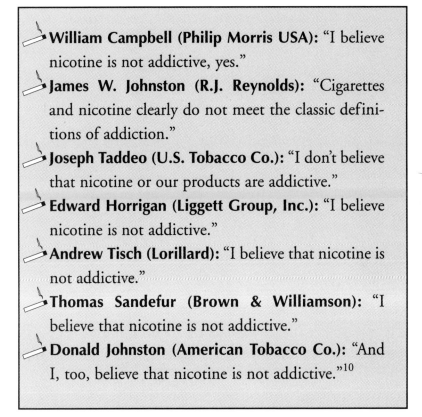

William Campbell (Philip Morris USA): "I believe nicotine is not addictive, yes."

James W. Johnston (R.J. Reynolds): "Cigarettes and nicotine clearly do not meet the classic definitions of addiction."

Joseph Taddeo (U.S. Tobacco Co.): "I don't believe that nicotine or our products are addictive."

Edward Horrigan (Liggett Group, Inc.): "I believe nicotine is not addictive."

Andrew Tisch (Lorillard): "I believe that nicotine is not addictive."

Thomas Sandefur (Brown & Williamson): "I believe that nicotine is not addictive."

Donald Johnston (American Tobacco Co.): "And I, too, believe that nicotine is not addictive."[10]

Unlike many others who watched the televised hearing on C-SPAN (a cable TV channel), William Farone knew for sure that these tobacco executives were lying. He had worked as a scientist at Philip Morris from 1976 to 1984 on the development of a "safe" cigarette. In 1994, Farone secretly gave information about the inner workings of the tobacco company to officials at the FDA. Later he would cooperate with trial lawyers on pending tobacco cases.[11]

How was Farone regarded for his disclosures about the tobacco industry practices and research? A government official

During a 1994 congressional hearing, executives of the nation's biggest tobacco companies made startling denials about the harm cigarettes are known to cause.

who worked with him said, "Farone was the diamond." But a Philip Morris attorney portrayed him as "a typical whistle-blower," a disgruntled former employee with "a motive to fabricate and to distort evidence through his hindsight."[12]

Several whistle-blowers disclosed important internal documents from Brown & Williamson. They were Merrell Williams, Stan Glantz, and Jeffrey Wigand. As a direct result of the damaging information they made available, the following outcomes were made possible:

- A Florida jury in the *Castano* case (see page 87) held the tobacco company responsible for a smoker's lung disease.

- Attorney General Mike Moore of Mississippi and attorneys general of other states sued the tobacco industry for Medicaid costs for ill smokers and won a huge settlement.

- The FDA declared nicotine a drug and sought to regulate the cigarette makers.

It all began with Merrell Williams. Williams worked as a paralegal (a lawyer's aide) for Brown & Williamson's law firm from 1988 to 1992. He secretly copied thousands of the tobacco company's internal papers and eventually turned them over to Richard Scruggs and Mike Moore. Scruggs passed them on to Congressman Waxman, who was holding congressional hearings on the tobacco industry in 1994.

Dr. Stan Glantz, was a heart doctor at the University of California, San Francisco. He received some of the tobacco company's internal documents from an unknown source a short time after the tobacco executives testified in 1994. Dr. Glantz said the documents revealed hard evidence about the tobacco company's research in nicotine addiction as well as smoking-related diseases and safer cigarettes.[13] One particularly damaging statement, for example, was made in 1963 by the company's top lawyer. He stated that "Nicotine is addictive. We are, then, in the business of selling nicotine, an addictive drug."[14]

A year later, the California Supreme Court ruled against Brown & Williamson's motion to suppress the information.

The next day, Dr. Glantz made the secret documents available to the world by posting them on the Internet. (This information can be found in "The Cigarette Papers Online" at http://www.library.ucsf.edu/tobacco/.)

Jeffrey Wigand gave damaging inside information about Brown & Williamson to the FDA in May 1994. Wigand had been vice president for research and development at the tobacco company from 1989 to 1993. In August 1995, he taped an interview with Mike Wallace for the television show *60 Minutes*. CBS's six-month delay in airing the interview became a controversial news story, which served to publicize the existence of the Brown & Williamson documents. Wigand then testified in the Mississippi Medicaid lawsuit in November 1995. The paper trail of the tobacco industry's self-incriminating documents was now complete.

Liggett Revisited—A New Attitude

In an astounding turnaround, one tobacco company official made unique compromises against the entire tobacco industry in the mid-to-late 1990s. Though not actually a whistle-blower, Bennett S. LeBow was an independent thinker. He was (and continues to be) the chairman and chief executive officer of Brooke Group Ltd., which acquired control of Liggett in 1986.

First, Liggett Group settled in the *Castano* case in 1996. In 1997, LeBow testified in the *Broin* case that cigarettes do cause cancer. He was the first tobacco executive to make this admission.

Also in 1997, LeBow obeyed a Massachusetts law requiring cigarette companies to reveal the ingredients of their brands of cigarettes to the public. Liggett was the first tobacco company to do so. "People have a right to know what's in their cigarettes," LeBow explained.[15] Other

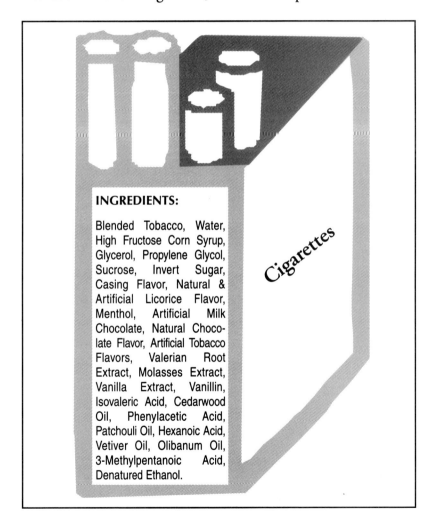

INGREDIENTS:

Blended Tobacco, Water, High Fructose Corn Syrup, Glycerol, Propylene Glycol, Sucrose, Invert Sugar, Casing Flavor, Natural & Artificial Licorice Flavor, Menthol, Artificial Milk Chocolate, Natural Chocolate Flavor, Artificial Tobacco Flavors, Valerian Root Extract, Molasses Extract, Vanilla Extract, Vanillin, Isovaleric Acid, Cedarwood Oil, Phenylacetic Acid, Patchouli Oil, Hexanoic Acid, Vetiver Oil, Olibanum Oil, 3-Methylpentanoic Acid, Denatured Ethanol.

Cigarettes

tobacco companies fought the law in court. They argued that ingredients of cigarettes are trade secrets. Therefore, the companies believed they should not be forced to reveal such information.

Then, between 1996 and 1998, Liggett settled tobacco lawsuits with attorneys general in forty-one states who sued to recover smokers' Medicaid costs.

As part of the multistate settlements, the tobacco company agreed to the following:[16]

- to acknowledge publicly that cigarette smoking is addictive

- to add a warning label on cigarette packs: "Nicotine is Addictive"

- to acknowledge publicly that cigarette smoking causes disease

- to acknowledge that they targeted the youth market (including children under the age of eighteen)

- not to oppose the FDA's regulations on tobacco

- to pay 25 percent of its pretax income over twenty-five years to the states

Why did LeBow go against the rest of the tobacco industry? He was motivated by financial concerns. LeBow explained that "Liggett could not afford to lose any" of the numerous lawsuits it would face under other conditions.[17] Liggett held only 2 percent of the cigarette market in the United States.[18] Stock analysts believed that LeBow wanted to reduce Liggett's financial debts in order to make the company more attractive for sale to another company. Then, in 1999, Liggett sold three of its cigarette brands (L&M, Lark, and Chesterfield) to Philip Morris for $300 million. Eve is Liggett's only remaining brand.

Other Weapons in the War on Tobacco

The war on tobacco continues to this day. In many cities, smoking is banned in public places, such as sports stadiums, public beaches, restaurants, and office buildings.

There are also federal, state, and local taxes on cigarettes. The taxes produce extra money while discouraging people from smoking. Also, the decrease in the number of smokers, in effect, reduces related health-care costs.

By 1930, federal tax money from tobacco products exceeded $500 million, of which 80 percent came from cigarette sales.[19] In 1997, the annual tax dollar amount from the sale of cigarettes was over $5.6 billion.[20] Federal taxes on cigarettes rose from eight cents a pack in 1951 to twenty-four cents a pack in 1993.[21] In 1999, Congress voted down President Clinton's proposal for a fifty-five-cents tax increase on cigarette packs. State taxes on cigarette packages vary widely by state. As of May 2000, these taxes range from 2.5 cents per pack in Virginia to one dollar per pack in Alaska.[22]

Despite the antismoking efforts by government and health officials and the widely publicized information about

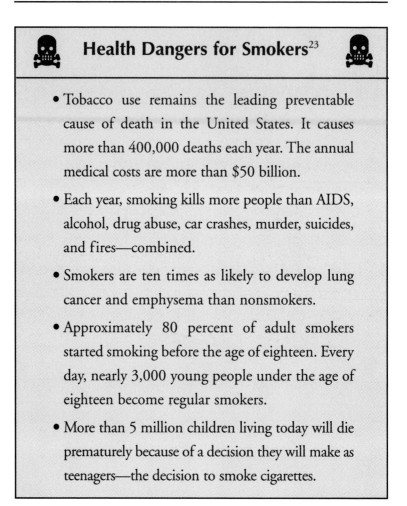

☠ Health Dangers for Smokers[23] ☠

- Tobacco use remains the leading preventable cause of death in the United States. It causes more than 400,000 deaths each year. The annual medical costs are more than $50 billion.

- Each year, smoking kills more people than AIDS, alcohol, drug abuse, car crashes, murder, suicides, and fires—combined.

- Smokers are ten times as likely to develop lung cancer and emphysema than nonsmokers.

- Approximately 80 percent of adult smokers started smoking before the age of eighteen. Every day, nearly 3,000 young people under the age of eighteen become regular smokers.

- More than 5 million children living today will die prematurely because of a decision they will make as teenagers—the decision to smoke cigarettes.

the serious health risks of smoking, Americans continue to smoke. Alarming health statistics associated with cigarette smoking continue to mount.

Other antismoking efforts were targeted specifically at young people. These efforts included not only stricter

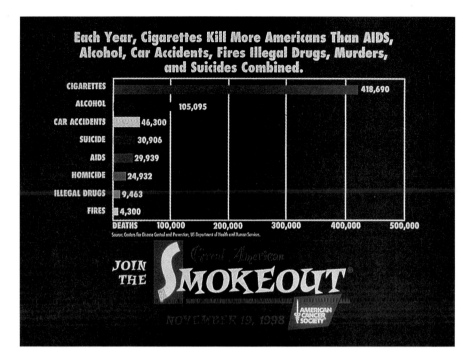

Cigarettes have killed more people each year than AIDS, alcohol, drug abuse, car crashes, murder, suicides, and fires—combined.

government regulations but also antismoking campaigns by nonprofit groups.

All fifty states prohibit the sale of cigarettes to minors (children under the age of eighteen). As of February 28, 1997, federal regulations require store clerks to check identification of anyone under the age of twenty-seven who wishes to purchase cigarettes. State requirements are even tougher, and often include the threat of fines.

The Campaign for Tobacco-Free Kids is the largest private antitobacco group. The more than one hundred organizations

Profile of High School Smokers (1997–1998)[24]

- 70.2 percent of students have tried cigarette smoking.

- More than one third (36.4 percent) were current smokers.

- White students (19.9 percent) were more likely than blacks (7.2 percent) or Hispanics (10.9 percent) to smoke frequently.

- About 90 percent of all new smokers are age eighteen and younger.

- More than one million teenagers started smoking in 1998. One third of them will die from their addiction.

in this nonprofit group include health and teacher groups and the National Parent-Teachers Association. The American Cancer Society sponsors The Great American Smokeout. It dedicates a week of activities each year to educate teenagers about the hazards of smoking.

Joe Camel

Why do many teenagers today pick up the smoking habit? One reason is the presence of cigarette advertising. The American Cancer Society reported that teens are twice as likely to be influenced by cigarette advertising than by peer pressure.[25] The Centers for Disease Control reported that tobacco companies spent $6 billion, or $16 million a day, on advertising and marketing in 1998.[26]

R.J. Reynold's ads that featured Joe Camel (from 1988 to 1998), a cool cartoon figure, are a notable example. In a *USA Today* survey conducted in early 1997, 95 percent of the respondents said they were familiar with the Joe Camel ads. Another study showed that six-year-olds were as familiar with Joe Camel as with Mickey Mouse.[27] Though the ads did not necessarily prompt teens to smoke Camels, they did influence teens to pick up the smoking habit.

In the 1994 Supreme Court decision of *Mangini* v. *R.J. Reynolds*, the Court supported a ruling by a California appeals court to allow Janet Mangini to sue R.J. Reynolds over its Joe Camel ads.[28] Mangini had filed a complaint in state court in January 1992 against the tobacco company. She argued that the Joe Camel promotional campaign, including mugs and matchbooks, did not carry health warnings.

In 1997, R.J. Reynolds settled with Mangini as the trial date neared. The tobacco company agreed to phase out Joe Camel ads and to release internal documents about its campaign to target the youth market.

Pregnancy and Smoking

One of the federally required warning labels on cigarette packs (as of 1987) targets pregnant women who smoke. It reads:

Smoking By Pregnant Women May Result in Fetal Injury, Premature Birth, and Low Birth Weight.

Research has shown that pregnant mothers who smoke may also have excessive bleeding or miscarriages. Premature or underweight babies are often at risk for developmental and health problems.[29]

The President and the FDA Get Tough

In 1995, the Food and Drug Administration (FDA) declared nicotine (one of the ingredients in tobacco) a drug. President Bill Clinton then approved the FDA's proposals for regulating the sale and marketing of cigarettes and other tobacco products to minors. The proposals would also give the agency the authority to regulate cigarettes as a "drug delivery device."[30]

Were the FDA's actions to regulate cigarettes legal? Though a district court judge upheld them, the U.S. Court of Appeals for the Fourth Circuit overturned the decision in 1998. "Congress never intended to give the FDA jurisdiction over tobacco products," the appeals court determined.[31]

Since all fifty states had already banned the sale of cigarettes to minors (anyone under age eighteen), the issue over the FDA rules was whether the FDA overstepped its authority. Brown & Williamson said that the rules were an example of "government overreaching."[32]

On April 26, 1999, the United States Supreme Court agreed to review the appeals court's ruling against the FDA.

The Court acted on a request by the Clinton administration. The Court heard oral arguments in the *FDA* v. *Brown & Williamson Tobacco* case on December 1, 1999.

Solicitor General Seth P. Waxman argued the FDA's position. (A solicitor general is a law officer appointed to assist an attorney general.) Waxman stated that cigarettes are the only dangerous products that remain unregulated by any federal agency. Richard M. Cooper, who represented R.J. Reynolds, argued the tobacco industry's position. "There is more at stake here than health," he stated. Cooper added that "economic markets" and "informed adult choice" go beyond the scope of the FDA.[33]

Another issue in this case was the official role of the FDA. The FDA's main role has been to make sure that food and drug products are safe and dependable. Suppose the FDA were allowed to control tobacco products. If tobacco was an unsafe drug, as the FDA claimed, then all products containing nicotine would have to be banned.

On March 21, 2000, the Supreme Court handed down a ruling in the case of *FDA* v. *Brown & Williamson*.[34] The decision found that the FDA does not have the legal power to control tobacco products.

Expensive lawsuits, settlements with states, taxes on cigarettes, and public opinion have weakened the tobacco industry. It is now up to Congress to determine their future.

Lessons & Legacies of the *Cipollone* Case

What lessons have we learned from the *Cipollone* case and beyond? Surely, we know the dangers of cigarette smoking today. We know how some well-intended laws for smokers were used as a shield by the powerful tobacco industry. We know the challenges of the difficult, costly, and lengthy legal battle that the Cipollones waged.

Clearly, the various legal arguments won and lost by the Cipollones provided a road map for other injured smokers and their families to use later in their own lawsuits. The tobacco industry documents that the Cipollone attorneys were able to uncover during the trial were invaluable in later tobacco cases. The *Cipollone* case raised important legal issues. Also, it inspired tougher regulations of the tobacco industry.

The *Cipollone* case put both smokers and the tobacco industry on notice. But, of the hard lessons of smokers' responsibilities as well as rights, what have we learned? What legacy did Rose Cipollone leave? You must be the judge.

Questions for Discussion

1. Before the *Cipollone* case, how did tobacco companies use cigarette warning labels as a form of protection from lawsuits?

2. Imagine that you are a Justice of the Supreme Court deciding the *Cipollone* case. You need to interpret both the 1965 Labeling Act and the 1969 Act. Did either or both of these laws shield the tobacco companies? Or, did either or both of these laws make them liable for the health consequences of smokers such as Rose Cipollone? Explain.

3. How serious a legal issue is the tobacco industry's hiding of evidence of the health hazards of cigarette smoking?

4. Do you think the current warning labels on cigarette packages and in ads deter new smokers? Do they influence smokers with longtime habits to quit?

5. Why do you think teenagers today smoke cigarettes, despite all the health warnings?

6. Does peer pressure influence more young people to smoke or to stop smoking?

7. Would higher taxes on cigarettes help teenage and/or adult smokers cut back on cigarette smoking?

8. Where do you stand on the issue of free choice v. nicotine addiction regarding cigarette smokers?

9. Cigarette makers have claimed that cigarettes have a calming effect on smokers. It means that cigarettes act as a tranquilizer, which is a drug. How would you respond to the tobacco industry on this issue?

10. If cigarettes were to be sold as drugs, should they be made by drug companies rather than by tobacco companies?

11. Should the FDA have complete authority to regulate cigarettes as a drug?

12. Should the government protect minors but not adults from smoking? Or, should adults be free to pursue unsafe habits like smoking so long as the habit does not harm others? What about the dangers of secondhand smoke to nonsmokers?

13. Considering the serious health hazards associated with cigarette smoking, what is the best action that the federal government should take?

    a. ban cigarette advertising
    b. control the sale and advertising of cigarettes
    c. restrict exports on cigarettes and other tobacco products
    d. ban the sale or purchase of cigarettes regardless of age
    e. other action (Explain your answer.)

Chapter Notes

Introduction

1. David Margolick, "Antismoking Climate Inspires Suits by the Dying," *The New York Times*, March 15, 1985, p. Bl, col. 3.

Chapter 1. Big Tobacco

1. *Cipollone* v. *Liggett Group, Inc.* 644 F. Supp. 283 (D.N.J. 1986).

2. Gene Borio, "History of Tobacco, Part IV," © 1997, Tobacco BBS, History Net, <www.historynet.com> (January 27, 1999).

3. Borio, "History of Tobacco Part II."

4. "Tobacco Industry Profile 1997," <www.tobaccoresolution.com>, (March 11, 1999).

5. Borio, "History of Tobacco Part III."

6. John Maxell, "Premiums Up," *Tobacco Reporter*, March 1996, p. 16.

7. Youth Media Network, Tobacco News Service, "January 1999 News Briefs," <www.ymp.org> (April 7, 1999).

8. Borio, "History of Tobacco Part III."

9. Frontline Online, "Inside the Tobacco Deal," © 1998 PBS Online and WGBH/FRONTLINE, <www.pbs.org> (March 15, 1999).

10. Stephen Koepp, "Tobacco's First Loss," *Time*, June 27, 1988, Lexis-Nexis; Amy Singer, "They Didn't Really Blame the Cigarette Makers," *The American Lawyer*, September, 1988, Lexis-Nexis.

11. Carl Scheraga and John E. Calfee, "The Industry Effects of Information and Regulation in the Cigarette Market: 1950–1965," *Journal of Public Policy & Marketing*, vol. 15, no. 2, Fall 1996, p. 216.

12. Ibid.

13. Borio, "History of Tobacco Part IV;" Gaylord Shaw, "Supreme Court Joins Fray over Tobacco," *Newsday*, p. A19.

14. Borio, "History of Tobacco Part III."

15. Common Cause News © 1996, 1997, Common Cause, <www.commoncause.org> (January 28, 2000).

16. The Tobacco Institute, December, 1992: "Tobacco Activity at the Federal, State and Local Levels—1992; Priorities for 1993."

17. Borio, "History of Tobacco Part IV."

18. "Tobacco Industry Profile 1997," <www.tobaccoresolution. org> (March 11, 1999).

19. Common Cause News © 1996, 1977, Common Cause <www.commoncause.org> (January 28, 2000).

Chapter 2. Building a Case

1. Marc Z. Edell, "Cigarette Litigation: The First Wave," *Tort and Insurance Law Journal*, vol. 22, Fall 1986, p. 90; Karen E. Meade, "Breaking Through the Tobacco Industry's Smoke Screen: State Lawsuits for Reimbursement of Medical Expenses," Volume 17, *Journal of Legal Medicine*, beginning at page 113 (1996) 17 J. Legal Med. 113 (1996).

2. Ibid.

3. *Pritchard* v. *Liggett & Myers Tobacco Co.*, 295 F.2d 292 (3d Cir. 1961).

4. Meade, p. 113.

5. *Cooper* v. *R.J. Reynolds Tobacco Co.*, 234 F.2d 170 (1st Cir. 1956).

6. *Lartigue* v. *R.J. Reynolds Tobacco Co.*, 317 F.2d 19 (5th Cir. 1963).

7. *Ross* v. *Philip Morris and Co.*, 328 F.2d 3 (8th Cir. 1964).

8. Meade, p. 113.

9. Office on Smoking and Health, U.S. Dept. of Health, Education, and Welfare, Smoking and Health, Report of the Advisory Committee to the Surgeon General of the Public Health Service (1964).

10. Centers for Disease Control, CDC TIPS Tobacco Information and Prevention Sourcepage, ©1999 <www.cdc.gov/tobacco> (January 1, 2000).

11. Federal Cigarette Labeling & Advertising Act of 1965, Pub. L. No. 89-92, 72 Stat. 282 (1965).

12. Meade, p. 113.

13. Dr. Elizabeth M. Whelan, "Cigarettes, Lawsuits and the United States Supreme Court," American Council on Science and Health (ACSH) publication, vol. 3, no. 4, 1991, <www.asch.org> (October 23, 1998).

14. Public Health Cigarette Smoking Act of 1969 Pub. L. No. 91-222, 84 Stat. 87 (1970).

15. Ibid.

16. Deposition of Rose Cipollone, January 26, 1984, p. 136.

17. Ibid., February 26, 1964, p. 346.

18. Adrienne Knox, "Rutted Road for Tobacco," *The Star-Ledger* (Newark, N. J.), April 7, 1991, Westlaw.

19. Deposition of Rose Cipollone, February 28, 1984, pp. 352–353.

20. 1990 U.S. Briefs 1038, October Term, 1990-May 23, 1991, amicus curiae brief of the six former surgeon generals of the United States, the American Council for Science and Health, and the Tobacco Products Liability Project, Lexis-Nexis. Also: Federal Trade Commission, Report to Congress, Pursuant to the Federal Cigarette Labeling and Advertising Act, June 30, 1967.

21. Deposition of Rose Cipollone, February 28, 1984, p. 346.

22. Comprehensive Smoking Education Act of 1984, Pub. L. 98-474, October 12, 1984, 98 Stat. 2200.

23. Deposition of Rose Cipollone, January 27, 1984, p. 271.

24. Gene Borio, "History of Tobacco Part III," © 1997, Tobacco BBS, History Net, <www.historynet.com> (January 27, 1999).

25. "Smoking Is Addictive, U.S. Surgeon General Asserts," May 20, 1988, Facts on File News World News Digest, *Facts on File News Services,* 1997, <www.facts.com> (April 7, 1999).

26. Ibid.

Chapter 3. The Road to the Supreme Court

1. Kevin R. Richardson, "Dying Woman, Attorney Make Unlikely David to Smite Cigarette Goliath: Industry Used Many Legal Stratagems in Its Attempts to Undermine Lawsuit," *The Star-Ledger* (Newark, N. J.), June 25, 1992, Westlaw.

2. Steve Nelson and Marge Olson, "Cigarette Product Liability Cases," *Legal Times,* December 9, 1985, Litigation Monitor, p. 8. Also: *Cipollone* v. *Liggett Group,* 593 F. Supp. 1146 (D. N. J. 1984).

3. Richardson.

4. Ibid.

5. Deposition of Rose Cipollone, January 26, 1984, pp. 14–71.

6. Ibid.

7. Ibid., January 27, 1984, p. 198.

8. Ibid., pp. 276–277.

9. Ibid., March 1, 1984, p. 470.

10. Ibid.

11. Ibid., January 26, 1984, pp. 129, 132.

12. Ibid., February 28, 1984, p. 424.

13. Richardson, [no page provided].

14. *Herbstman* v. *Eastman Kodak Co.,* 68 N.J. 1, 342 A.2nd 181, (1975).

15. C. F. Fenswick, "Cipollone v. Liggett Group, Inc.: Supreme Court Takes Middle Ground in Cigarette Litigation," *Tulane Law Review,* vol. 67, February 1993, p. 787.

16. Al Kamen, "Tobacco Industry Wins Protection from Some Lawsuits; Cigarette-Pack Notices May Preclude Claims," *The Washington Post*, January 13, 1987, p. A11.

17. Frank Tursi, Susan E. White, and Steve McQuilkin, *Lost Empire: The Fall of R.J. Reynolds Tobacco Company*, Chapter 28, Part 2, "A Privilege Denied," © *Winston-Salem Journal*, <www.journalnow.com> (January 18, 2000).

18. Morton Mintz, "Supreme Court Allows Release of Evidence in Cigarette Suit," *The Washington Post*, December 8, 1987, p. C3.

19. Stephen Koepp, "Tobacco's First Loss," *Time*, June 27, 1988, Lexis-Nexis.

20. Deposition of Rose Cipollone, January 27, 1984, p. 270.

21. "Chronology of Cipollone Case," United Press International, June 14, 1988, © 1988, U.P.I., Lexis-Nexis.

22. Deposition of Rose Cipollone, January 26, 1984, pp. 136, 145–146, 158.

23. Ibid.

24. Ibid.

25. "Widely Watched Tobacco Case Enters Final Round," Reuters, June 6, 1988, Lexis-Nexis.

26. *Cipollone v. Liggett Group, Inc.*, 683 F. Supp. 1487 (D. N. J. 1988).

27. Alan M. Darnell and Meryl G. Nadler, "323 Important Rulings Emanating from the Cipollone Tobacco Trial," *California Western Law* Review 1988–1989, Westlaw. Also: *Cipollone v. Liggett Group, Inc.*, 683 F. Supp. 1487 (D. N. J. 1988).

28. James Eli Shiffer, "Tobacco Researchers Say They Were Searching for a Safer Smoke," *The News and Observer* (Raleigh, N. C.), July 15, 1996, p. A1.

29. *Cipollone v. Liggett Group, Inc.*, 644 F. Supp. 283 (D. N. J. 1986).

30. Mary Griffin, "The Smoldering Issue in Cipollone v. Liggett Group, Inc.: Process Concerns in Determining Whether Cigarettes Are a Defectively Designed Product," *Cornell Law Review*, vol. 73, March 1988, p. 606; *Cipollone* v. *Liggett Group, Inc.*, 644 F.Supp. 283 (D. N. J. 1986).

31. Deposition of Rose Cipollone, January 27, 1984, p. 268.

32. *Cipollone* v. *Liggett Group, Inc.*, 683 F. Supp. 1487, (D. N. J. 1988).

33. Amy Singer, "They Didn't Really Blame the Cigarette Makers," *The American Lawyer*, September 1988, p. 31.

34. Ibid.

35. Ibid.

36. Ibid.

37. Ibid.

38. *Cipollone* v. *Liggett Group, Inc.*, 693 F. Supp. 208 (D. N. J. 1988).

39. Singer, p. 31.

40. Thomas C. Galligan, Jr., "Product Liability—Cigarettes and Cipollone: What's Left? What's Gone?" *Louisiana Law Review*, vol. 53, January 1993, p. 713.

41. Singer, p. 31.

42. Ibid.

43. Andrew Blum, "Tobacco Litigation: Cipollone and Its Progeny," *The National Law Journal*, December 26, 1988, p. 20.

44. Frank Tursi, Susan E. White, and Steve McQuilkin, *Lost Empire: The Fall of R.J. Reynolds Tobacco Company*, Chapter 28, Part 2, "A Privilege Denied," © *Winston-Salem Journal*, <www.journalnow. com> (January 18, 2000).

Chapter 4. The Arguments for Cipollone

1. Written comments of William K. Suter, Clerk of the Supreme Court.

2. Ibid.

3. "Supreme Court to Tackle Death-from-Smoking Suit," *The Record*, March 26, 1991, p. A01.

4. Ibid.

5. Tracy Schroth, "U.S. High Court Grants Cert in Cipollone," *New Jersey Law Journal*, April 4, 1991, p. 4.

6. 505 U.S. 504, 509–10 (1992).

7. No. 90-1038, 1990 U.S. Briefs 1038, October Term, 1990-May 24, 1991, Brief for Petitioner.

8. Ibid.

9. 1990 U.S. Briefs 1038, October Term, 1990-May 23, 1991, Brief of the American Medical Association as Amicus Curiae in Support of Petitioner, Lexis-Nexis.

10. Robert Cohen, "High Court to Rehear Arguments in Jersey Smoking Liability Case," *The Star-Ledger* (Newark, N. J.), October 22, 1991, Westlaw

11. No. 90 1038 Supreme Court of the United States, 1991 U.S. Trans Lexis 214, October 8, 1991, Washington, D.C.

12. Robert Cohen, "Court Rules for Jersey Family, 'Unshields' Tobacco Industry," *The Star-Ledger* (Newark, N. J.), June 25, 1992, Westlaw.

13. Schroth, p. 4.

14. Ibid.

15. Robert Cohen, "Court Rules for Jersey Family, 'Unshields' Tobacco Industry," *The Star-Ledger* (Newark, N. J.), June 25, 1992, Westlaw.

Chapter 5. The Arguments for Liggett Group, Inc.

1. No. 90-1038, 1990 U.S. Briefs 1038, October Term, 1991-June 10, 1991, Brief for Respondent.

2. Ibid.

3. Ibid.

4. No. 90-1038, 1990 U.S. Briefs 1038, October Term, 1991-June 10, 1991, Brief of the National Association of Manufacturers as Amicus Curiae in Support of Respondents.

5. No. 90-1038, 1990 U.S. Briefs 1038, October Term, 1991-July 10, 1991, Brief Amicus Curiae of the Association of National Advertisers, Inc., in Support of Respondents, Lexis-Nexis. Also: Pub. L. No. 89-92, 79 Stat. 282, reprinted in 1965 U.S. Code Cong. & Admin. News 300.

6. C. F. Fenswick, "Cipollone v. Liggett Group, Inc.: Supreme Court Takes Middle Ground in Cigarette Litigation," *Tulane Law Review,* vol. 67, February 1993, p. 787.

7. No. 90-1038, 1990 U.S. Briefs 1038, October Term, 1991-June 10, 1991, Brief for Respondent.

8. Robert Cohen, "High Court to Rehear Arguments in Jersey Smoking Liability Case," *The Star-Ledger* (Newark, N. J.), October 22, 1991, Westlaw.

9. Ibid.

Chapter 6. The Decision

1. Isodore Starr, *The Federal Judiciary* (New York: Oxford Book Company, 1961), p. 36.

2. *Lindsey* v. *Tacoma-Pierce County Health Dept.*, 8 F. Supp. 2d 1213, (W. D. Wash. 1997); *McCulloch* v. *Maryland,* 17 U.S. 316, 427, 4 L. Ed. 579 (1819).

3. Sheila Birnbaum and Gary E. Crawford, "How Cipollone Affects Other Industries," *The National Law Review*, August 24, 1992, section: Business Watch; Torts; p. 20.

4. *Cipollone* v. *Liggett Group Inc.*, 505 U.S. 504, 516, (1992).

5. *Cipollone* v. *Liggett Group Inc.*, 505 U.S. 504, 516 (1992).

6. Robert Cohen, "Court Rules for Jersey Family, 'Unshields' Tobacco Industry," *The Star-Ledger* (Newark, N. J.), June 25, 1992, Westlaw.

7. Ibid.

8. Ibid.

9. Ibid.

10. Ibid.

11. John Riley, "New Door to Smoker Suits; High Court OKs Damages Based on Deception or Hidden Data," *Newsday*, June 25, 1992, p. 4.

12. Ibid.

13. Kathy Barrett Carter, "Lawyers Predict Little Change in Liability Case. High Court Ruling in Cigarette Suits Brings About Wait-and-See Attitude," *The Star-Ledger* (Newark, N. J.), June 28, 1992, Westlaw.

14. "Deep Pockets," *The Star-Ledger* (Newark, N. J.), December 10, 1992, Westlaw.

15. Larry C. White, "Laundering the Profits of Tobacco," *St. Petersburg Times*, November 16, 1988, Lexis-Nexis.

16. *Cipollone* v. *Liggett Group, Inc.*, 140 F.R.D. 681; 1992 U.S. Dist. LEXIS 1809; 60 U.S.L.W. 2544.

Chapter 7. Where We Stand Today

1. Robert Cohen, "Court Rules for Jersey Family, 'Unshields' Tobacco Industry," *The Star-Ledger* (Newark, N. J.), June 25, 1992, Westlaw.

2. "The Cigarette Wars: Stop Smoking!" *Economist*, vol. 339, no. 7965, May 11, 1996, pp. 21–23.

3. Campaign for Tobacco-Free Kids, "A Chronology of Events in the War on Tobacco," August 1995-November 1996; © 1997, National Center for Tobacco-Free Kids, <www.tobaccofreekids.org> (October 24, 1998).

4. *Engle* v. *R.J. Reynolds Tobacco Co.*, #94-08273-CA-20 (Dade County Ct., filed May 5, 1994).

5. *Cancer Facts & Figures 1999*, American Cancer Society, Inc. © 1999, p. 26.

6. Scott Olsen, "Indy Tobacco Case Begins as Florida Man Gets Award," *The Indiana Lawyer*, August 21, 1996, p. 1.

7. "Inside the Tobacco Deal: Timelines," 1998 PBS Online and WGBH/FRONTLINE, <www.pbs.org> (March 15, 1999).

8. *Henley* v. *Philip Morris Inc.*, No. 995172, 1999 WL 221076, (Cal.Super. April 6, 1999) p.1.

9. "$81M Smoking Verdict: Jury Sides with Family of 3-Pack-a-Day Man," Combined News Services, *Newsday*, March 31, 1999, p. A8.

10. John Schwartz, "Reengineering the Cigarette," *The Washington Post*, January 31, 1999, p. W08. Also: "Inside the Tobacco Deal: Nicotine and Cigarettes," 1998 PBS Online and WGBH/FRONTLINE, <www.pbs.org> (March 15, 1999).

11. Schwartz, p. W08.

12. Ibid.

13. "The Cigarette Wars: Stop Smoking!" *Economist*, vol. 339, no. 7965, May 11, 1996, pp. 21–23.

14. Ibid.

15. Martin Finucane, "Despite Injunction, Liggett Discloses Cigarette Ingredients," The Associated Press, December 16, 1997, <www.onlineathens.com> (January 7, 1999).

16. Campaign for Tobacco-Free Kids, "Chronology of Events in the War on Tobacco," August 1995-November 1996, © 1997.

17. Timothy Noah, "OK, OK, Cigarettes Do Kill," U.S. News, March 31, 1997, © *U.S. News & World Reports*, Inc, U.S. News Online, <www.usnews.com> (April 7, 1999).

18. Ibid.

19. Gene Borio, "History of Tobacco, Part III," © 1997, Tobacco BBS, History Net, <www.historynet.com> (January 27, 1999).

20. Centers for Disease Control, CDC TIPS Tobacco Information and Prevention Sourcepage, 1999, <www.cdc.gov/tobacco> (January 1, 2000).

21. "Smoking," Microsoft® Encarta® 97 Encyclopedia. © 1993–1996 Microsoft Corp.

22. MSNBC, "State by State," <www.msnbc.com> (April 24, 2000).

23. *Cancer Facts & Figures-1999*, American Cancer Society, Inc. © 1999, p. 25. Also: "Growing Up Drug Free," October 23, 1998, U.S. Department of Education, Washington, D.C.

24. *Cancer Facts & Figures-1999*, American Cancer Society, Inc. © 1999, p. 25.

25. American Cancer Society: Great American Smokeout FAQ, <www.cancer.org> (October 26, 1998).

26. Centers for Disease Control, CDC TIPS Tobacco Information and Prevention Sourcepage "State Laws on Tobacco Control—United States, 1998" Fact Sheet, <www.cdc.gov/tobacco> (January 16, 2000).

27. Borio, "History of Tobacco Part IV."

28. *R. J. Reynolds* v. *Mangini*, 513 U.S. 1016 (1994).

29. "Growing Up Drug Free," October 23, 1998, U.S. Department of Education, Washington, D.C.

30. Borio, "History of Tobacco, Part IV."

31. Gaylord Shaw, "Supreme Court Joins Fray over Tobacco," *Newsday*, April 27, 1999, p. A19; *Brown & Williamson Tobacco Corp.* v. *Food & Drug Admin.*, 153 F. 3d 155 (4th Clr. 1998).

32. Ibid.

33. Tony Mauro, "Justices Skeptical of FDA Bid to Regulate Tobacco," *Legal Times*, December 2, 1999, Law News Network, <www.lawnewsnetwork.com> (December 2, 1999).

34. *Brown & Williamson Tobacco Corp.* v. *Food & Drug Admin.*, 153 F. 3d 155 (2000).

Glossary

appeals court—A court of law that has the power to review the decision of another, lower court.

breach of warranty—A violation of a maker's or seller's written or oral promise.

brief—A written argument in a legal case.

charge—The final address by a judge to the jury before it carefully discusses and decides the issues in a case in order to reach a verdict.

circuit court—A federal circuit court has authority over states. There are thirteen courts of appeal in the federal court system.

civil lawsuit—Legal action relating to private rights and damages.

class-action lawsuit—A case in a court of law brought by a group of people with common complaints. There is a single trial.

common law—A set of rules and principles relating to the government and security of persons and property. Common law gets its authority only from usage and custom. It is different from statutory law, which is passed by lawmakers.

concur—To agree with the conclusions or the results of another Justice's opinion filed in a case, though not necessarily with the same reasoning.

cross-examine—Questioning of a witness by the opposing party.

damages—Money that is awarded as compensation for a loss or injury.

defendant—The person who is sued in a civil lawsuit or the person accused of a crime in a criminal prosecution.

deposition—A pretrial, formal interview with a witness during which the witness gives testimony under oath.

discovery—A pretrial search for information and documents that apply to a case. Tools of discovery may include: depositions, written questions, and questions concerning physical or mental conditions.

express warranty—A written or oral advertising promise.

implied warranty—An advertising promise stated indirectly.

jury instructions—A judge's statement to the jury concerning the rules or principles of law that apply to the case.

lawsuit—A legal action between two parties in a court of law.

liability—A broad legal term applied to obligations or debts for which someone is responsible. (See also *product liability* and *strict liability*.)

litigation—A legal action or lawsuit.

motion—A formal request for a judge to issue a decision about a matter before the court.

negligence—In a civil lawsuit, the breach of a duty of care that causes damages to a person.

opinion—A written explanation of the court's decision.

petitioner—A person who begins a court proceeding.

plaintiff—The party who is suing someone else in a civil lawsuit.

plurality—The opinion in which a larger number of justices join than not. A plurality opinion is not a majority opinion.

preemption—Having precedence over. It is a legal principle applied to certain matters of great national importance where federal laws take precedence over state laws.

product liability—The legal liability of makers and sellers to compensate buyers and users for damages suffered because of product defects.

respondent—The defendant at the Supreme Court level.

strict liability—Liability without fault. It is a concept applied in product liability cases.

testimony—Evidence given by a competent witness who is speaking under oath. This type of evidence is distinguished from evidence taken from writings and other sources.

"with prejudice"—A dismissed case cannot be reactivated at a later date.

writ of *certiorari*—An order by an appeals court to hear the appeal of a particular case from a lower court. Also, the United States Supreme Court, at its choosing, may grant a petition to review a case.

Further Reading

Brigham, Janet. *Dying to Quit: Why We Smoke and How We Stop.* Washington, D.C.: National Academy Press, 1998.

Fahs, John. *Cigarette Confidential: The Unfiltered Truth About the Ultimate American Addiction.* New York: Berkley Publishing Group, 1996.

Haughton, Emma. *A Right to Smoke?* New York: Franklin Watts, Inc., 1997.

Hilts, Philip J. *Smokescreen: The Truth Behind the Tobacco Industry Cover-Up.* Reading, Mass.: Addison-Wesley Longman, Inc., 1998.

Hyde, Margaret O. *Know about Smoking.* New York: Walker & Co., 1995.

Kluger, Richard. *Ashes to Ashes: America's Hundred-Year Cigarette War, the Public Health, and the Unabashed Triumph of Philip Morris.* New York: Knopf, 1996.

McGurn, Barrett. *America's Court: The Supreme Court and the People.* Golden, Colo.: Fulcrum Publishing, 1997.

Miller, Marvin. *The Best of You Be the Jury.* New York: Scholastic Inc., 1999.

Mollenkamp, Carrick, Adam Levy, Joseph Menn, and Jeffrey Rothfeder. *The People vs. Big Tobacco: How the States Took on the Cigarette Giants.* Princeton, N. J.: Bloomberg Press, 1998.

Orey, Michael. *Assuming the Risk: The Mavericks, the Lawyers, and the Whistle-Blowers Who Beat Big Tobacco.* New York: Little, Brown, 1999.

Petrone, Gerard S. *Tobacco Advertising: The Great Seduction*. Atglen, Pa.: Schiffer Publishing, Ltd., 1996.

Pringle, Peter. *Cornered: Big Tobacco at the Bar of Justice*. New York: St. Martin's Press, 1998.

Quiram, Jacquelyn. *Alcohol and Tobacco—America's Drugs of Choice*. Wylie, Tex.: Information Plus, 1997.

Whelan, Elizabeth. *A Smoking Gun: How the Industry Gets Away With Murder*. Philadelphia: George Stickley Co., 1984.

Internet Addresses

ABCNEWS.com, Big Tobacco Under Siege, <http://www.abcnews.go.com/sections/US/DailyNews/tobacco616_timeline.html> (October 11, 2000).

CNN.com, Focus: Tobacco Under Attack, "A Brief History of Tobacco," <http://www.cnn.com/SPECIALS/1998/tobacco/history/> (October 11, 2000).

Frontline Online, Inside the Tobacco Deal, "1983–Rose Cipollone and Judge Lee Sarokin," <http://www.pbs.org/wgbh/pages/frontline/shows/settlement/timelines/cipollone.html> (October 11, 2000).

Rebecca Kurson, "Philip Morris Has Smoker's Cought," *Green* magazine, <http://www.greenmagazine.com/2000/01/000113b.asp> (October 11, 2000).

Index

126

Public Health Cigarette Smoking
   Act (1969), 21, 33, 66, 71,
   77, 81, 82, 85
R
Raulerson v. *R. J. Reynolds Tobacco*,
   91–92
Rehnquist, Chief Justice William,
   71, 79, 82
R. J. Reynolds, 14, 16, 27, 88, 89,
   92, 105
Ross v. *Philip Morris Inc.*, 28, 29
S
Sarokin, Judge H. Lee, 18, 47, 48,
   54, 56, 57, 59, 63
Scalia, Justice Antonin, 71, 79
Scruggs, Richard, 89, 97
secondhand smoke, 89–90
Slaughter, Edward, 84
Souter, Justice David H., 71, 79,
   82
states' Medicaid lawsuits, 89, 100
Stevens, Justice John Paul, 71, 79,
   81, 82
Surgeon General's "Report on
   Smoking and Health," 19,
   30–32, 34, 89
Surgeons General
   Koop, Dr. C. Everett, 36, 37
   Terry, Dr. Luther L., 30
T
tar, 17, 18
Thomas, Justice Clarence, 71, 79
tobacco industry
   Congress and, 14, 20, 35, 47,
      56, 71, 75, 77, 78, 81, 94,
      97, 101, 107

history of, 11–12, 14–24
internal documents, 49–52, 96,
   97–98, 105
lobby, 19–21, 37
Tobacco Institute, 18, 37, 88
Tribe, Lawrence, 71, 72, 73, 83
U
United States Constitution, 19, 50
United States Court of Appeals for
   the Third Circuit, 47, 49, 51,
   63, 67, 70, 75
United States Supreme Court, 28,
   49, 50, 64–66, 67, 74, 77,
   79–80, 106
   Justices of, 71, 79, 82, 83
W
Wall, Charles, 74, 76
Walters, Cynthia, 52
warning labels, 33, 34, 35, 36, 46,
   49, 57, 62, 66, 68, 70, 78, 82,
   100, 105–106
Waxman, Solicitor General Seth,
   107
whistelblowers, 94–97
   Farone, William, 945–96
   Glantz, Dr. Stanton, 96, 97–98
   Harris, Dr. Jeffrey, 55, 94
White, Justice Byron R., 71, 79,
   82
Whiteley v. *Raybestos-Manhattan*,
   93
Wigand, Jeffrey, 96, 98
Williams, Jesse, 93
Williams, Merrell, 96, 97
Wynder, Dr. Ernst, 17, 18